Ghost Stories of Atlantic City

And Other

Odd & Ghastly Tales

from the

World's Playground

Ghost Stories *of* Atlantic City

And Other

Odd & Ghastly Tales

from the

World's Playground

A. L. Reeser

Front cover: Steel Pier from the Boardwalk, by Kevin D. Margitich

1stSight Press
Monocacy, PA

First Printing 2010
Printed in the United States of America
ISBN 978-0-9729265-6-0

For Eileen, Anne, & Mary,
my links to Atlantic City

Table of Contents

Atlantic City has never been one to look back. The brainchild of a small town doctor, the "City by the Sea" that would become the showy behemoth of today was conceived in an era of Victorian modesty, in the 1850s. That no roads or rails led to this imagined health resort, that only seven modest dwellings — all but one owned by the same family — stood upon the otherwise wild and mosquito-infested island, that investors and legislators continually scoffed at the presumptuousness of the resolute doctor, never caused Atlantic City to pause. It is, perhaps, this tradition of headstrong determination to make something out of nothing that has been both the bane and the bounty of the town.

A dizzying ascent to success culminating after World War II, followed by many false starts, has left scant evidence on the Boardwalk of Atlantic City's past. Hotels have been repeatedly torn down for newer, bigger, and hopefully more appealing ones. Venues notorious for their celebrity patrons have vanished, and, in some cases, reincarnated elsewhere. Piers have washed away or burned down, replaced with structures hopefully better able to weather their perches above the sea. Yes, Atlantic City has its ghosts.

Beyond the Boardwalk and the dazzling casinos sprawls the rest of Atlantic City. Here, change perhaps has been harder to come by. Vestiges of bygone eras peer from behind newer facades, while old boardinghouses once buzzing with faithful summer visitors now stand bereft on barren city blocks. Elsewhere, the streets are reminiscent of Atlantic City's "Pennsylvania stepfather," as Philadelphia was called by a promotional magazine for Atlantic City, whose working classes were essential to the resort's success.

Both on the shore and off, Atlantic City has pressed on, mindful only of the present and the pursuit of future gains. The city has persevered, quietly at times, and despite the reputation that has dogged it since at least the 1960s. A recent visitor illustrated this reputation in a particularly trenchant article on the resort, painting it as no more than a sleazy mirage, choosing words such as lurid, cheap, gross, banal, and soulless to describe what he saw as merely a stage-set. Another, more benign, perspective from a longtime resident shows that it depends on how you look at it: Cheap and soulless become bewitching and audacious, sleazy and cheap become indulgent and flashy.

Of course, people continue to visit Atlantic City — variously known over the years as "The City by the Sea," "The World's Playground," and "The Queen of Resorts" — for some sort of respite. From its start as a health resort, through its long run as one of the first tourist destinations, up to its current role as a gambling mecca, Atlantic City has mastered the art of entertainment, forsaking, at times, its own history to provide a century's worth of memories to its visitors. Determined to stay abreast of The Tourist's whimsy,

Atlantic City as seen from the top of Absecon Lighthouse
Was the dream of a seaside health resort the
artful ploy of a salesman after all?

Atlantic City found its formula for success: romanticized illusions and the commercialization of amusement.

With all of the shape-shifting that Atlantic City's skyline has undergone, it would seem at first glance that there aren't many buildings or landmarks that have had a chance to become "historic," and, by extension, to boast a ghost story. It's widely believed that earthbound spirits attach themselves to a building or area that held importance to them in life, which seems incompatible with Atlantic City's ever-changing landscape and population. But to jump to this conclusion would be to underestimate the allure of Atlantic City. Fortunately for us, both the historic buildings that have been preserved, as well as the ones that remain only in spirit, have had their share of unexplainable phenomena and have their tales to tell.

At the cusp of Atlantic City's prime, in the late 1800s, another doctor, Dr. Thomas K. Reed, predicted the city's rise to iconic status in a prophetic tribute:

> ... it will be a city beautiful, and Atlantic avenue will be paved. With its population quadrupled and its wealth

> increased beyond the dreams of avarice, Atlantic City, because of its peerless climate, its incomparable location and its unrivalled attractions, will be then the capsheaf of all resorts the world over and the pride and glory of every American heart.

One look at the whirlwind of the famous, infamous, and anonymous fun-lovers, and of the nightclubs, restaurants, and theaters that have lined Atlantic City's Boardwalk and streets over the years, confirms that this city has had its finger on the nation's partying pulse for over a century.

Today, Atlantic City's risqué motto reflects its high-spirited objective: "Always turned on." Nevertheless, when the lights go out at night, spirits from the city's unforgettable past have been known to make unscheduled appearances. As they say, the show must go on.

Sometimes, however, when you begin to chip away at the plaster smiles and chiseled veneer, you find fame's murky cousin, infamy. So, along with tales of Atlantic City's famous come several remarkably odd stories of its infamous, whose legacies add a sinister snarl to the town's twisted history.

The forgotten legends and unsolved mysteries extend to Atlantic City's neighbors as well. The landscape just above Atlantic City forms a craggily network of interconnected waterways and islands of all different sizes. Bordered on the east by the biggest of these islands, Brigantine, the marshy maze's westernmost border is the mainland, which harbors the vast, thick, and eerily quiet Pine Barrens. Long before Atlantic City burst forth from reedy isolation, this backcountry made a perfect lair for the ne'er-do-well, the luckless, and the forsaken. Here, strange tales unfolded of spectral vigils, mooncussers, pirates, and one unloved, unearthly fiend, all of which hatched into enduring bits of folklore.

Atlantic City, circa 1917, by H.B. Smith
Library of Congress

It may well have been Dr. Jonathan Pitney, Atlantic City's founder, and his supporters who unwittingly opened the door to Atlantic City's legacy of hauntings. In the beginning, the railroad companies launched a national campaign to advertise the therapeutic idiosyncrasies of Atlantic City. Pamphlets could be found across the country extolling the healing properties of Atlantic City's ocean air. This air, particularly the unique component of ozone, virtually guaranteed "perfect health." A breath of fresh air, along with the mild weather brought by a peculiar shift in warm ocean currents that only favored Atlantic City, could be just what the doctor ordered. No one could argue that Atlantic City hasn't done its best to provide this therapy, whether by sun, sand, or cash. Rejuvenation, revitalization, and rebirth. Might these same hopes be the source of some of Atlantic City's ghost stories? Make no mistake: Beyond the world of the thrill-seekers, sun-worshippers, and faithful residents of the "City by the Sea" is a hidden, secret world — a "city of the dead." A world of elusive phantoms, mysterious apparitions, and familiar ghosts whose summers never ended.

An old lifeless boat guarding the weeds

Dr. Pitney's House: Death's Serenade

If one day you happen to take the back way to Atlantic City, before you reach the grassy estuaries of Absecon Bay, turn off the highway toward the small town of Absecon. Amid the updates expected over the course of many centuries, history still breathes through the many clapboard houses dating from the town's early days. Driving by these old country homes with their wrap-around porches and white picket fences, you can imagine you are watching the flickering images of an old movie reel, where everything seems awash in an idle, sepia-toned, summertime haze.

One of the oldest roads in Absecon is Shore Road, which was constructed in 1716 by English colonists and now hugs the mainland coast under various pseudonyms for thirty miles from Somers Point to just past Leeds Point. Originally called "King's Highway," Shore Road follows an already well-worn path, one used for years by the Lenni Lenape Indians to travel to their summer lodgings on Absecon Island, the piece of land that now holds Atlantic City, Margate, Ventnor, and Longport.

Along the ancient throughway of Shore Road sits the house of Dr. Jonathan Pitney, who is fondly regarded as the "Father of Atlantic City." His home is a beautiful structure from the 1800s, beckoning to passers-by from its perch close to the road. It has an aura of invitation about it, and an air of authority as well, as if it absorbed the characteristics of the popular and trustworthy Dr. Pitney.

Dr. Jonathan Pitney
Absegami: Annals of Eryen Haven
& Atlantic City

It's not uncommon for houses like this, which not only have witnessed so much history but also have been renovated, to have supernatural phenomena occur. But the haunting in the vicinity of Dr. Pitney's old house doesn't follow the course of most ghost stories. That said, if you do find yourself on this well-traveled road, listen for the faint sound of a fife. Local lore has it that guests of the Jonathan Pitney House, which is now a bed and breakfast, have heard the haunting music when they thought they were the only ones present.

In truth, the key to this haunting may not have anything to do with Jonathan Pitney. The spirit may not have been anyone he knew or was close to; he might not even have been aware of the person's passing. But the haunting could have had something to do with why it was from this house in Absecon that Jonathan Pitney was inspired to create Atlantic City. It is here, five marshy miles away from the island, where the odd legend begins of how a veritable sanctuary was transformed into the World's Playground.

Absecon sits just across Absecon Bay from Absecon Island, the home of Atlantic City. This location gave Absecon ringside seats to the island's fabled transformation from wilderness to wild city. Absecon Island remains unique in that it has been a summer destination for quite some time — 14,000 years by some estimations of Lenni Lenape history. The Lenni Lenape Indians settled all of New Jersey and parts of New York, Pennsylvania, and Delaware. They lived according to the seasons, and, in the summer, seafood and birds' eggs were plentiful on the shore and could be dried for winter consumption. These original seasonal guests of the island called it *Absegami*, meaning "Little Sea Water," a word that gives us the modern-day "Absecon." The Lenni Lenape eventually moved westward, selling the last of their land rights to New Jersey in 1832 for $2,000.

The idea of permanently settling on the desolate beach didn't appeal to many people. What with the greenheads, the mosquitoes, the snakes, and the storms, the island certainly lacked the creature comforts one would expect in a year-round home. In the late 1600s, a Quaker farmer, Thomas Budd, invested in property on both sides of Absecon Bay, reportedly purchasing the land from a group of English whalers. It's said he leapt at the chance to unload his purchase, selling parcels on the mainland for forty cents per acre and on the beach for a mere four cents per acre.

Some time after Thomas Budd left, and after the pirates seeking shelter came and went, and after army deserters from the Revolutionary War came and went, the Leeds family came to settle quite happily on Absecon Island. Around the turn of the nineteenth century, Jeremiah Leeds chose the island for his family's homestead. Where some might have seen desolation, Leeds saw tranquility. Where others might have seen acres upon acres of useless sand, he saw fields of rye and corn and grazing land for his profitable steers. The snarls of trees and thorny bushes meant an abundance of fruit and berries to the practical father of ten.

By 1850, Jeremiah's descendents still lived on Absecon Island, although with less enthusiasm than their industrious patriarch it seems. Farming had become dull, and the remaining Leeds had grown lukewarm to their inheritance. Their ambivalence proved a boon to the men, one of whom was Jonathan

Pitney, who were eyeing the entire island as a potential cash crop.

Dr. Pitney arrived in Absecon sometime between 1819 and 1820. Having recently completed medical school and a two-year assistantship at a hospital on Staten Island, the young twenty-something rode into town on horseback, carrying nothing but a blanket, some clothes, and his medical supplies. A few years later, he purchased a relatively new colonial-style home, built in 1799 by Samuel Reed.

Like many of us, Pitney desired a room with a view. It logically occurred to him that if his house were taller, he would be able to view the Absecon shoreline at his leisure. Strangely enough, instead of simply building onto the original structure, he cut his house in half, removed the northern part, and transferred it to his backyard. In its place, he built a three-story, Italianate-style addition with a cupola on its roof. No matter how it came to be, Pitney now had his view.

Not long after, an entrepreneurial spirit grasped hold of Dr. Pitney. Inspiration blew in on the warm bay breeze. *A splendid resort town — no, a city!*

View of Atlantic City from Absecon

— something like Cape May, only bigger...and better! A health retreat, of course! Warm sun and fresh, ocean air...who wouldn't concede to the benefits of a weekend by the sea? Especially if a doctor tells them so!

That Pitney and his investors managed to follow through with these seemingly audacious plans was remarkable, especially given the question posed by a skeptical legislator: *Who needs a railroad to nowhere?* And this unwavering ambition raises another question: What motivated Pitney to persevere despite the huge obstacles they faced? Perhaps he was frustrated that his medical career had become unfulfilling and remained unprofitable, despite his loyal patients. Maybe he was disappointed by his short-lived political career...he had rather recently lost the race for House Representative. Or maybe he was just tired of his financial position in life (his mother-in-law reportedly supplemented his small income).

Or, perhaps Pitney's motivation lay in his own mortality, in leaving a legacy before he died, in needing a *raison d'être*. Deep in thought, he would have observed the bay between himself and Absecon Island from the front of his house. But had he turned in the other direction, he would have had a birds-eye view of the cemetery next to Absecon United Methodist Church. Is there any motivator more powerful than coming face to face with death?

This is where, late at night, the faint sound of the fife is heard. Although the origins of the ghostly music remain a mystery, the cemetery is a likely candidate. Dating back to 1796, the churchyard is the eternal resting place for hundreds of old New Jersey families, among them many Civil War soldiers – Sergeants, Captains, and Privates who served in New Jersey, Pennsylvania, New York, Maryland, and possibly other infantries. The fife and drum were present in virtually every aspect of the soldiers' lives, governing every daily activity on and off the battlefield. Historians say that for veterans of the Civil War, no other sound recalled the war like those of the fife and drum, and the sound of the fife, according to Civil War Field Music historian David Poulin, would have been akin to nails on a chalkboard, a "nauseating" sound.

The Civil War was the deadliest conflict in United States' history, with an estimated 620,000

Cemetery at Absecon United Methodist Church
Although cemeteries are not, as one might expect, the most common places for hauntings, they have always been considered potential doorways to the spirit world, known as portals. Since ancient times, people have believed that sites associated with death or intense emotions, and often secluded or lonely sites, serve as passageways for spirits of the dead entering the world of the living.

deaths. Attending the all-too frequent funerals became one of the most common chores for the fife and drum musicians, and the honors were strictly laid out by military code. As described by Bruce and Emmett's *The Drummers' and Fifers' Guide* (1862), the funeral procession would begin with the corpse escorted by two ranks. To the beat of solemn music, the escorts marched the coffin slowly toward its grave. During the actual burial, the fife and drum were silent. Not until the escorts were outside the boundary of the cemetery would the music resume. At this point, as if in defiance of the bloodshed they had seen and in celebration that they were still alive, the musicians would break into the jolly, upbeat tune "Merry Men Home from the Grave."

Could the haunting fife music heard today be a replay of a military funeral procession from long ago, when a fifer stepped outside the cemetery and tried to allay the mourning with music? Why would such a

> Unexplainable noises are one of the most common experiences in reports of paranormal activity. These mysterious sounds can take the form of songs, footsteps, knocks, bangs, and rustles. Other sensory forms of spirits include smells, coldness, and "invisible" touches.

scene replay hundreds of years later?

One possibility arises with the story of Jonas Somers, who served in New Jersey's 10th Infantry, known for its admirable record in 33 battles. According to Alfred Heston's history of the area, Somers died in 1864 in a hospital in Philadelphia. Friends evidently "removed" him from Philadelphia to the Absecon cemetery. It's possible that Somers fought in the Battle of Cold Harbor in 1864, noted by General Grant as being one he regretted most due to the amount of casualties suffered by the Union troops after a horrific frontal assault by the Confederates. If Somers died as a result of wounds sustained in this battle, perhaps the lingering fife music originates from the day he was laid to rest. An untimely death is a frequent cause for hauntings, as are feelings of regret, which might have accompanied Somers' passing.

The grave marker of Jonas Somers in the Absecon cemetery

Heston's annals makes mention of other soldiers buried in the Absecon cemetery as well. William Adams, who served in a Maryland battery, was killed in Atlantic City when he fell from a scaffold. Frederick Kirchenman, from a Pennsylvania regiment, died by gunshot in South Atlantic City. Sergeant William Pine fought with the 11th Company B New York Infantry, which fought in the famed Battle of Bull Run, and his life was claimed by a nitroglycerin explosion. Had all of these men escaped death during the war, only to die once they returned? Perhaps the uncanny sound of the fife we hear today echoes from one of these darkly ironic deaths.

Whether Jonathan Pitney ever ran into the ghostly fifer in this area is unknown. Nevertheless, this is where he dreamed up the legendary Atlantic City, in this little old town across the bay, from the third story of his house, which he built specifically to view the shore. Here, Dr. Pitney gazed out to the coast, and with death ever-present behind him, he reincarnated himself as the "Father of Atlantic City."

Absecon Lighthouse at Graveyard Inlet

The night is inky black; the darkness seems impenetrable. Clouds obscure the moon and stars. Rain comes in sheets. Lightning briefly illuminates a frantic crew scurrying across the hull of a hapless ship off the coast. Water pours on deck as the ship's underbelly momentarily appears in one particularly precarious tilt. The ocean makes a plaything out of the ship, tossing, twisting, oblivious to the gravity of its antics.

Before the storm began, you watched approvingly as the ship carefully navigated the coast. But now, as it approaches the northern part of the island, you fear the worst. Has the captain heard of the deadly shoals of Absecon Inlet? Does he know about the thousands of people who lost their lives here?

You close your eyes and steady yourself for the impending wreck. For the unforgivable sense of helplessness. For the impact and the ripping apart of wood and metal. For the terrible sound of chaos. Screams. Cries. The moans of a mortally wounded boat. A horrifying cacophony of man versus sea. Pieces of masts, decks, and railings scattered. Corpses drifting among the ruins, sinking unhurriedly to their sodden graves in Graveyard Inlet.

You wait but hear nothing. You slowly open your eyes. The ship has passed unharmed. How easily you forget how much time has gone by! If it were back in your time, back before the lighthouse, the ship surely would have joined the hundreds of others here in the inlet. Once the lighthouse came, though, the wrecks stopped. The consecutive flashes in the sky defeated those sneaky shoals. (On your watch, you always thought that the ships looked like they were nodding back to you, bobbing up and down at the sight of the trusty beacon.) You look behind you through the glass window to the lighthouse light. It's dark nowadays, unneeded. But you remain here, just in case. Watching from your implausible position on the top of the lighthouse. A keeper of the light in life — now, a sentinel in the dark.

Absecon Lighthouse looms over the northern end of Atlantic City, not on the beach, as you might expect, but curiously situated among a hodgepodge of empty lots, apartment buildings, hotels, and houses at Rhode Island and Pacific Avenues.

As massive symbols of safety and protection, visible for miles around, lighthouses have always drawn people to them, both the living and the lifeless. There are hundreds of reportedly haunted lighthouses around the world, all with their own fascinating stories ranging from the quaint to the downright frightening. But one lighthouse you won't easily find on these lists — at least not yet — is Absecon Lighthouse. A televised paranormal investigation in the lighthouse yielded little results, evidently due to bad weather. But for those in the know, Absecon Lighthouse has proven to be a very active place.

Some people say there are over a dozen spirits haunting this lighthouse. Most of the sightings take the form of victims from shipwrecks off the coast in Graveyard Inlet, with one particularly persistent account of the apparition of a Revolutionary War soldier who lost his life nearby. This soldier was probably on board the *Mermaid*, which was passing through on March 31, 1779, from Halifax to New York when it wrecked off the coast. It took 31 hours for rescuers to reach the ship, at which point they saved 42 troops and crew. More than 145 people from the ship perished, either from drowning or from freezing to death in the cold March waters. This type of tragedy was not an uncommon occurrence in the days before the lighthouse.

Another well-known legend places the spirit of a man at the top of the lighthouse, arms extended toward the sea. Those who have witnessed this apparition feel the earthbound spirit appears to warn ships about the dangerous waters of Absecon Inlet. Could these onlookers have stumbled upon a lightkeeper from long ago, one of the dedicated few whose spirit has returned to carry on the oath of vigilance and protection? Volunteers working on the ground floor have reported hearing the clinking of footsteps on the iron steps of the tower, all the while knowing they were the only ones in the building. The significance of these footsteps will become clear later in our story.

First illuminated in 1857, the lighthouse came into being by the untiring efforts of Atlantic City's beneficent forefather, Dr. Jonathan Pitney, who probably had seen firsthand the devastation wrought by the shoals between Brigantine and Atlantic City. According to Jack E. Boucher's history of the island, the area's notorious reputation dates all the way back

Volunteers also believe they have a ghost who leaves dimes throughout the museum section of the Keepers Quarters. The dimes are always found in unusual places, not by the cash register, as one might expect. Another source reports the sound of voices coming from overhead. An explanation has never been found, but those who have heard them say they sound like merry spirits.

to 1695, when it came to be known as Graveyard Inlet due to the deaths caused by the peculiarly located sandbars beneath the water. Pitney's petitions for the lighthouse began in the mid-1830s, and even after Congress determined there was insufficient evidence in favor of one, he persevered. In the meantime, more than sixty shipwrecks added to Absecon Beach's already impressive roster of wrecks.

Not until the packet ship *Powhattan* ran aground April 16, 1854, at Long Beach, which is twenty-five miles north of Atlantic City, did officials reconsider their earlier decision. All on board, the crew plus 311 German emigrants, lost their lives that night when a terrible nor'easter blew in. The wreckage and bodies washed ashore all down the Jersey Coast, with some of the corpses surfacing at the North Carolina Avenue beach in Atlantic City (the site of Resorts Hotel and Casino today). Pitney again pleaded with Congress, pointing out that the fatal wreck may

Not all shipwrecks brought tragedy. In the early years, the "Robert Morgan" became beached at the foot of New York Avenue. The ship stayed there for five months, becoming a temporary tourist attraction. Thousands had the pleasure of paying 10 cents to walk on her decks. She eventually dislodged from the sand, and floated away.

never have happened if there were a lighthouse to guide their way. That same year, Congress finally appropriated $35,000 for the construction of a lighthouse at Absecon Inlet. When it was completed and the lantern was lit on January 15, 1857, Absecon Lighthouse's kerosene flame could be seen almost 20 miles out to sea. Not another ship wrecked for 10 months.

Absecon Lighthouse safeguarded Jersey's waters for over 70 years, eventually being decommissioned in 1933. During that time, the lightkeepers were the ones who dedicated their lives (and their families') to the upkeep of the building. Their most important task was making sure the light at the top of the tower stayed lit and the glass lens around it stayed clean. As we've seen, people's lives depended on it. These were grueling tasks, tended to every single night from dusk until dawn, and during the day as well. Preparation for the night ahead usually began at 10:00 a.m., which meant, in the days before an electric light was installed, the lightkeeper had to haul the fuel to the top of the lighthouse, enough to keep the lantern lit all night. A total of 240

Steps leading to the top of Absecon Lighthouse

steps ascended from the ground level to the lantern room. And that's only one trip!

Needless to say, when people today hear unexplainable footsteps echoing off the iron steps in the tower, the lightkeepers of decades ago come to mind first. There were a total of six men who served as principal lightkeepers over the course of the lighthouse's operation. The first was Daniel Scull, appointed in 1856 and paid a yearly salary of $600. The last was Knud Hansen, who left office in 1930. In between were William Bartlett, John S. Nixon, Abraham G. Wolf, and Thomas Bills.

Major Abraham G. Wolf was the longest serving keeper of the light in Atlantic City. He dedicated twenty-three years of his life to guarding the waters of Absecon Bay, eventually transferring to a newly built lighthouse on Squaw Island in Michigan.

> In addition to its task of aiding sailors, Absecon Lighthouse realized early on that opening its doors to tourists could benefit both the lighthouse itself and the tourism industry of Atlantic City, which was in high swing in the early 1900s. They were right. In 1912, the lighthouse held the title of "Most Visited Lighthouse in America," welcoming over 10,000 visitors in a three-month period. This legacy continues, and the lighthouse remains one of Atlantic City's historic gems.

Three events stand out from the time he spent in Atlantic City: an earthquake, the loss of a loved one, and a near-death experience. The earthquake occurred August 30, 1886, during his thirteenth year on the job. As if experiencing an earthquake was not unsettling enough, afterward, he also feared he was the only one who had felt it. His account of that night survives in the logbook all keepers were required to maintain:

> August 30, 1886, 9:52 p.m. — Felt a shock of earthquake while on top of tower. Pipes in closet rattled as if a gale of wind were blowing. The tower swayed so I could hardly keep my footing. The wind was north-northwest, very light, and it was cloudy and smoky both. Motion, north to south. Duration, about one minute. I was out on the gallery at the time. Came in and looked at the clock. Had difficulty in doing so. Could not have left it if I had wished to do so, and I think I did at the time.

Following this incident on the tower, he called down to his wife Kate, who was in the kitchen at the time. She hadn't felt a thing, and suggested he had merely experienced vertigo. The assistant keeper, who came to relieve Wolf at 10:00 p.m., also hadn't felt any shocks. When the assistant saw that Wolf had logged the quake in the book, he delicately advised to rub it out. If Wolf was the only person to feel it, the assistant reasoned, perhaps their superiors would think Wolf had lost his mind. Not until the next morning, when the newspaper confirmed that an earthquake had struck, were Wolf's fears put to rest.

Two years later, Major Wolf's wife died. The notice in the paper read, "ATLANTIC CITY, July 29. —

In 1833, Keeper Wolf was interviewed about the tendency of birds to fly too close to the lantern room of the Absecon Lighthouse. Too often, a gust of wind would smash them right into the glass, leaving a bloody mess. Even after he installed a wire mesh around the glass, birds still died. Once, a large duck collided with the mesh, denting it before falling dead to the ground. Another time, a large snipe flew with such force into the netting that it sheared its feathers off. Nonetheless, Wolf admitted that such unfortunate occurrences supplied him with a bountiful dinner table. He may not have been aware that birds in general, and especially those that fly into windows and houses, are universal death omens. Superstition also holds that they are possessed by the souls of the dead.

Mrs. Kate W. Wolfe, wife of Major G. Wolfe, the well-known lighthouse keeper of Atlantic City, died this afternoon after a long and painful illness." Her death was momentous enough to the editors to include it in the same story as the daily resort count, as the next paragraph relayed that the city remained "in perfect order" amid its 24,000 visitors.

Seven widowed years later, Major Wolf was involved in a bizarre, near-fatal accident, a wreck of sorts, but this one in downtown Atlantic City rather than out at sea. The Beach Casino, located at the end of Baltic Avenue, unexpectedly and disastrously collapsed in on itself while hosting an Elks reunion with thousands of attendees. Wolf was one of the first ones dug out from the catastrophic wreck, unconscious and badly injured. Headlines screamed: "INTO A PIT OF DEATH, Thousands of Elks Go Down in a Collapsing Building, Two Hundred Hurt." Rumors spread that the building had been condemned weeks before. Eyewitness accounts told of how the floor joists suddenly gave way, leaving no time for the hundreds gathered to get out of harm's way. Despite his serious injuries, Wolf survived the accident. Not long after this near-death experience,

Wolf left Atlantic City for a new lighthouse in the Midwest. Would his spirit be the one to return to the lighthouse after the freakish and tragic things he experienced in Atlantic City? Maybe.

But there are two more possibilities. Captain Thomas Bills, the second-to-last keeper of Absecon Lighthouse, died in November of 1914 after eighteen years of service. A death notice reported that Bills died "a martyr to duty." Evidently, Bills had recently suffered an illness or injury that required surgery in a Philadelphia hospital. Unwilling to be away from the lighthouse any longer than he already had been, he insisted on returning to work over his doctors' objections. He should have listened to them. In a terrible twist of fate, on his way home to Atlantic City, he suffered a relapse and lost consciousness. He was rushed home to the lighthouse, where he soon died.

Captain Bills was not the only keeper to die here. William Bartlett, the second principle lightkeeper, was appointed to the post at Absecon Lighthouse in 1861 by then-President Abraham Lincoln. He served only four years before he died. A brief notice in the newspaper stated that Bartlett died of paralysis. The cause went unstated.

Many believe hauntings occur because people leave behind something they feel they must return to, whether that something is unfinished business, unspoken words, or something else neglected or imperfectly left behind. There is no telling what location a spirit may choose to haunt, but usually, it is one to which they have a deep-seated connection, good or bad. Case in point is the prevalence of ghosts from the shipwrecks here in Graveyard Inlet seen seeking solace in the steadfast beacon. But the story behind the apparition at the top of the tower — the one facing the ocean, the one fiercely watching over the coastline — perhaps that story belongs to one of the lightkeepers from long ago who died on his own watch.

As any ghost would surely tell you, change is inevitable. Even still, it is well known that renovations of any kind can disturb spirits who, up till then, have been slumbering peacefully. Perhaps the construction jolts them out of an otherworldly sleep, or perhaps the

According to a 1930s guide to New Jersey, sea gulls portend good luck to fishermen of southern New Jersey, but killing them would invite the severest of bad luck. In Irish lore, the souls of drowning victims inhabit seagulls.

impending change is enough to snatch them back from wherever they dwell in the spirit world. Indeed, there is another chapter in Absecon Lighthouse's history that bears mention, and perhaps owes its bittersweet outcome to a little help from the Other Side. In 1998, in the middle of a long-anticipated restoration project, a fire broke out at the lighthouse in the early morning dawn. A police officer came across the blaze while on patrol and quickly dispatched the fire company. By the time the fire trucks arrived, the Keepers Quarters were in ruins, totally ravaged by the flames.

The committee had decided to rebuild the Keepers Quarters exactly as they were when the lighthouse was decommissioned in 1933. Unfortunately, the construction up to the point of the fire left the wood framing exposed, which became veritable kindling for the blaze that swept through. All that the fire fighters could do was pour water on the tower to impede the path of the fire.

The tower itself had just been completed a week earlier. The finishing touches had been placed on the lantern room, which is the glass enclosure at the top of the lighthouse that houses the light. They later discovered that the metal door that sealed the Keepers Quarters from the bottom of the tower was closed tightly, preventing the fire from spreading up the steps. As if by miracle, the entire tower remained unharmed.

Recovering from their sadness and frustration, the members of the lighthouse committee slowly picked up the pieces, and renovations eventually resumed. Now the Keepers Quarters stands fully restored at the base of the lighthouse, a tribute to the lightkeepers who lived there in its attention to detail.

Of the many ghosts of the lighthouse, one spirit surely rests a little easier. That is, until that spirit sees a ship out to sea, passing dangerously close to Graveyard Inlet, and it once more reaches toward the ocean in a futile attempt to warn the ship of the deadly shoals hidden beneath the water.

Lucy the Elephant: Back from the Dead

"The only elephant you can walk through and come out alive." So reads the offbeat motto on old brochures for Lucy the Elephant — a six-story, wood and metal, elephant-shaped building that looks out over the Atlantic Ocean. And while it's probably safe to assume Lucy is the only elephant you can walk through, period, whether everyone milling about Lucy is among the living, well, that might be a different story.

Lucy is inarguably one of the most outlandish, and somehow most endearing, landmarks you will ever stumble upon. She passes her days just off the beach on Atlantic Avenue in a town once known as South Atlantic City, now called Margate. From her howdah sixty feet off the ground, you can see miles of coastline in either direction: Atlantic City and Ventnor to the north, Longport and Ocean City to the south. But her view of the beach is only one of the interesting things about her. A staircase contained in one of her rear legs takes you into her hollowed-out belly, a beautiful pink cavern housing relics from her past.

While she is well past retirement age (she's pushing 130 now), chances are, she's far from calling it quits. Given all she has seen and experienced, though, it wouldn't be surprising if she did.

James V. Lafferty, Jr., a real estate speculator from Philadelphia, designed Lucy in 1881 as a real estate office and as a way to lure people to the conveniently located, yet quietly situated, South Atlantic City. The elephant-shaped building had two equally important tasks – to draw attention to the area and to provide an aerial view of the island. She faired so well, Lafferty patented the whole idea of making anthropomorphic structures (he didn't want to limit himself to elephants) in 1882. Two other elephants eventually joined Lucy along the Atlantic Ocean – the Light of Asia in South Cape May and Elephantine Colossus in Coney Island. Lucy is the only one still standing.

This venture lasted until 1887, when the Gertzen family bought her. For the first time, she was an attraction unto herself; it cost ten cents to walk through her. Then, in the summer of 1902, the Gertzens rented Lucy to an English family who refurbished her interior with household amenities. A year later, Lucy found herself knee-deep in sand after a terrible storm and had to be moved back from the beach. Soon after, the Gertzens ventured into the slightly more daring world of booze, operating Lucy as a tavern until Prohibition.

Legend credits Sophia Gertzen, daughter-in-law of the man who bought Lucy, with naming the elephant. Sophia, in fact, was the last Gertzen to try to make a go of her. For awhile, Sophia ran a tourist camp around her, but city officials eventually shut it down. Undaunted, she opened a beer garden, then a

While Lucy has captured the hearts of many, a few heartless fools still mock her. In the 1970s, fraternity boys stole her tusks, perhaps in the interest of making her anatomically correct (only male elephants sport tusks). More recently, people have been known to throw bottles at her after *they've* hit the bottle.
They claim she moves.

hotel, next to Lucy. After Sophia died in 1963, her children donated their monstrous family heirloom to the city.

Through it all, Lucy submitted quietly, her shy smile fading with each passing season. The decade following Sophia's death saw Lucy deteriorate to a mere shadow of her former self. Withering, rusty, falling apart at the seams, she wore her drabness like a ratty coat. A thoughtless thwack could have knocked her down. What was once magnificent was now grotesque. Despite all she had witnessed in South Atlantic City, despite the famous people who had visited her over the years, no one could be bothered with her.

Almost by miracle, a committee of kind-hearted locals saved Lucy from the brink of extinction. The Margate Civic Association and the Save Lucy Committee planned to move her to prevent her demolition for new development, and once more Lucy narrowly escaped death. Three days before the move, however, a corporation owning land adjacent to Lucy's new site sought and received an injunction to stop it, claiming she would devalue their property. A judge agreed to a hearing the very next morning, something unheard of, and subsequently ruled that Lucy's move could proceed as planned. And it did, on July 20, 1970, just a couple of hours behind schedule. A thick, heavy fog blanketed the town, and Lucy patiently waited two hours to begin her once-in-a-lifetime journey. When the fog lifted, Lucy took a stroll down Atlantic Avenue, all ninety tons pulled by a small pick-up truck. Hordes of cheering people lined the street and followed the procession as Lucy gamely, and some say proudly, rolled down the street.

The dark days of despair before her relocation were not the only near-death experience Lucy survived. Back in 1904, when she operated as a tavern, she felt the cool, dank breath of death upon her neck and lived to tell about it. A careless patron overturned an oil lamp inside Lucy's wooden interior. That night, she almost burned to the ground.

Sources today claim an apparition appears in the pre-dawn hours in Lucy's howdah, with its feet kicked up and a drink in its hand. It is believed to be the spirit of a bartender from Lucy's tavern days, who enjoyed unwinding with a drink after work. Is the appearance of the barkeep a warning from the Other Side to keep a close eye on Lucy? Or maybe it is less ominous. Maybe it is simply a snapshot from Lucy's long, colorful past that has been superimposed on her present, for reasons unknown to all but Lucy and her ghostly visitor, who, contrary to the claims of Lucy's brochure, is most certainly not of the living.

The beach through Lucy's eyes

O Captain, My Ghostly Captain

View of Graveyard Inlet from the top of Absecon Lighthouse
The surfmen's precarious relationship with the sea was perfectly captured in the Life-Saving Station's deadly serious motto: "You have to go out but you don't have to come back."

At the turn of the last century, the folks in Brigantine, the town to the north of Atlantic City above Absecon Bay, were looking to make good use of their proximity to the new resort. In addition to building hotels and laying tracks straight to Philadelphia, they decided to try out the name North Atlantic City in hopes of luring the gamesome visitors of the Gay Nineties in their direction. The town's foray as North Atlantic City lasted only briefly, whence they weathered a century's worth of economic ups and downs. Today, it is a small, mostly residential community that is content to leave the frivolity of Atlantic City on the other side of the bay.

No doubt the dangerous shoals that prompted the construction of the Absecon Lighthouse have something to do with the appearance of a shadowy figure frequently seen on Brigantine's beaches. Old-time lore recounts a story of a drenched and wind-battered apparition who materializes ahead of storms and approaches passersby, imploring them to abandon the shore. Many times, recounts local historian William McMahon in his book of folklore, people have witnessed the mysterious figure vainly trying to speak to them over the din of the crashing waves.

Many superstitions accompany life by the sea. The bucca, or bucca-boo, from Cornish folklore, is a mischievous ocean spirit that dwells with fishermen. The prudent sometimes offer fresh fish, bread, and beer to pacify these spirits. Of the more earthly beliefs, traditional weather forecasting in New Jersey generally started from the ground up. If the morning brought no dew and many snails, or if fish leapt airborne and a cat cleaned its face, or if birds kept low to the ground, rain was approaching.

While the exact identity of this voiceless specter remains untold, most believe it is the spirit of a shipwrecked captain whose terrified expression bespeaks the horror he experienced at the hands of a raging sea. Some think the spirit's determination to warn those it encounters is tied to a grave failure of some sort on the captain's part. Either way, the scene always unfolds the same. A curious visitor goes to the beach to watch the storm approach. As the wind intensifies, the waves crash harder, and the clouds darken, the figure of an unkempt man in a long black coat takes shape. The phantom captain races up to the unsuspecting onlooker, waving its arms and soundlessly shouting. Although the veil invariably remains un-pierced, the long-ago captain rehearses these warnings again and again.

There is another possibility for the spirit's frequent reappearances. A lifelong seafarer, Atlantic City's beloved Captain Amasa Bowen worked for most of his life as a "surfman," or "wrecker," as they were sometimes called, one of the first to arrive at the scene

> For ten years, Brigantine Castle stood on the old Sea Horse Pier at 14th Street North. The legendary haunted attraction still haunts the memories of the millions who braved it.

of a shipwreck. When he was young, in the early nineteenth century, he worked under the direction of the first wrecking master, Ryan Adams, and later, after the establishment of the Atlantic City Life-Saving Station, he succeeded Adams as keeper, where he served the South Jersey shoreline until he was seventy-seven years old. According to Heston, Captain Bowen was quite the storyteller, always telling "thrilling accounts of the terrible loss of life that followed the failure of the wreckers to reach the helpless sailors." Heston also relates that there were times when there were up to six ships wrecked at one time on the beach, such was the formidableness of the Brigantine shoals.

Captain Bowen died just five years after he left his post at the Atlantic City Life Saving Station. In those five years, he took to chartering a yacht from Absecon Inlet. On one of these trips, a cold winter

Captain Amasa Bowen's brushes with death weren't limited to his job as a surfman. Twenty-odd years before he died, a band of thugs broke into the hotel he co-owned, the New Excursion House at Connecticut and Atlantic Avenues in Atlantic City, and nearly stabbed him to death. Bowen's daughter, Augusta, who evidently inherited her father's bravery, stood over the helpless Bowen, fending off the attackers.

day, he set off for Brigantine. He was found sometime later, floating aimlessly in the bay, almost frozen to death on the floor of his boat. He died from the exposure soon after.

Over the course of the next century, people would tell the story of a ghostly sea captain, dressed in an old black frock, windswept and weather-beaten, who haunted the shores here, his only message a silent cry of urgency to abandon the beach. Perhaps Captain Bowen's ghost remains on this island to forever haunt people with one last "thrilling" tale. His own.

The Vampiric Invasion of 1858

Sleeping was downright impossible. The buzzing, the swatting, the biting, and, worst of all, the unbearable itching. At night, the hotels smoked out their buildings, carefully covering the chimney and letting the smoke billow through the rooms and out the doors and windows. But it didn't work. The blood-thirsty mosquitoes and flies had too many in their flanks. There was nowhere to go to get away from them. Every hotel and boarding house on the island had tried the same thing, and some had even built bonfires outside, hoping a moat of flames would keep the enemy at bay. Peering out the window was like glimpsing a horrible nightmare, where horses lay in the streets, surrendered and bloodied, where cows walked right into the water without pausing. The entire island was under assault, and there wasn't another train until morning. This wasn't what anyone

> In Japanese folklore, mosquitoes are seen as reincarnations of the dead and known as *Jiki-ketsu-gaki*, or a blood sucking spirit. These souls find themselves in mosquito form as punishment for their wrongdoings in previous lives.

had in mind for their summer vacation.

What sounds like a B-rated horror movie, was, in fact, the PR nightmare of the newly inaugurated Atlantic City. Sure, there had been storms, train accidents, setbacks, and obstacles. But one thing they probably hadn't predicted was an invasion of vampiric bugs. In August of 1858, just one year after the resort town officially "opened," mosquitoes and greenhead flies assailed the town with such force, patrons were begging train conductors to take them off the island.

An article in a Philadelphia newspaper recounted some of the more peculiar incidents during the chaos. Near the inlet, a horse-drawn carriage was smashed to pieces when the horses went berserk from greenheads. One of the women in the carriage, a guest at the United States Hotel on Atlantic Avenue, broke her arm in the melee. Elsewhere, a group of men woke in the middle of the night, unable to sleep because of the creepy-crawlies, and went up and down the halls of the place they were staying, banging on all the doors loud enough to wake everyone. The men and women gathered in the parlor and voted unanimously to demand that the landlord install netting across all the doors and windows that very night.

What the locals already knew was that the low-lying marshes and ponds from the island's pre-development days were ideal breeding grounds for mosquitoes and flies, and the pests took full advantage of them. Although officials and landowners had made minor efforts to fill in the watering holes, it took them two years after this episode to make a concerted effort to rid the town of breeding grounds. An invasion of similar scale has not taken place since. But the Mosquito Plague of August of 1858 surely belongs in the record books as one of the most bizarre phenomena to descend on Atlantic City.

Mosquitoes as big as sparrows once terrorized European settlers in northern Jersey, according to a 1930s guide to New Jersey. As the story goes, mosquitoes were thought to make good hunting companions, paralyzing an animal until the hunter could shoot it. The Native Americans believed that blood from white men increased this skill and thus encouraged the bugs to bite the settlers, who in turn sought revenge by killing the Chief's horse. In the ensuing battle, the Indians summoned a battery of mosquitoes. Farther south, at the Manasquan River Inlet, a legend is passed around about a crew of men who were besieged by mosquitoes and had to hide under an iron kettle. Undeterred, the mosquitoes tried to reach them by piercing the kettle. The men took up their hammers and riveted each mosquito to the metal until the bugs just up and flew away with the whole kettle.

The Boardwalk:
An Otherworldly Playground

Atlantic City in 1870
Absegami: Annals of Eyren Haven & Atlantic City

There was no way to predict its overwhelming allure, perhaps because there was nothing with which to compare it in 1870. To those who promenaded shoulder-to-fashionable-shoulder, with hair smartly coiffed around faces glowing with excitement, the Atlantic City Boardwalk — all one mile of it at first, then two miles, then four by 1896 — held them spellbound. Friends, families, honeymooners, lovers, hucksters, peddlers, hagglers, bigwigs, all came together in one magnificent hullabaloo to stroll these wooden planks for two grim purposes: to have fun and to be noticed. Over time, the Boardwalk would be canonized in history books as the first of its kind, memorialized in countless postcards, and reminisced by millions, and it would take on various, even unflattering, trademarks: from awe-inspiring and luxurious to tawdry and vulgar. That is part of the Boardwalk's beauty. However, there is one word decidedly absent from memories of the Boardwalk's many attributes: Haunted.

That the Boardwalk harbors such a dark secret should come to no surprise given the legacy of one of its founders, Alexander Boardman, a train conductor and hotel proprietor during Atlantic City's formative years. Along with Jacob Keim, a fellow hotelier,

Atlantic City Boardwalk circa 1900
Absegami: Annals of Eyren Haven & Atlantic City

Boardman proposed, in 1870, the idea of a walkway along the beach for the practical reason of keeping sand out of the hotels and trains. The first Boardwalk (nicknamed Boardman's Walk) was a modest, temporary structure, only eight feet wide and collapsible so it could be taken in for the winter. The carnivalesque quality of today's Boardwalk was still years away; city ordinances prohibited any buildings at all along the Boardwalk at first. From these prudish Victorian beginnings, the Boardwalk swiftly claimed a place in the hearts of generations to come, even claiming international charm as "The World's Playground."

But for the Boardwalk's founding father, love was not so simple. In fact, legend has it that Alexander's amorous quandaries hold the seed to a tangled web of ghost stories that span two states and at least three towns.

In a small country town in Pennsylvania, locals tell a scandalous story involving Alexander's one-time summer house. Almost 100 years ago, Alex's ailing wife, later nicknamed Lizzie, was pushed down the stairs by her nurse (and soon to be replacement). But Lizzie was not so easily gotten rid of. To this day, her ghost continues to haunt the old abandoned farmhouse that witnessed her betrayal, targeting especially those visitors with dubious intentions. Sightings of a pale, wispy apparition have been accompanied by a range of mishaps, from uncomfortable feelings and minor injuries to car wrecks and suicides.

Alexander Boardman also owned buildings in Ocean City and Cape May, New Jersey, which *also* harbor stories of a mysterious spirit who appears as a whitish, vaporous, female figure. Some say that all three ghost stories derive from "Lizzie's" tragic death in Pennsylvania — that her spirit returns to the places she once lived to give an otherworldly voice to her mostly forgotten story. Others claim the paranormal phenomena occurring at these different locations are the work of three distinct ghosts. Nonetheless, one clear commonality remains: Alexander Boardman,

> Like a game of whisper-down-the-lane, many times the details of tales like this one become murky in the years of retelling. In doing further research on the Boardman legend, it appears likely that Alex's story might be a mash-up of different accounts involving several different people. One such person sticks out in particular, Alex's son Horace, who made headlines in 1906 for divorcing his wife and moving with his mistress to his boyhood home in the country.

and so, perhaps it was Alex's knack for attracting ghost stories that explains all of the Boardwalk's supernatural secrets.

The Fortune Teller's Curse

It may have done Mr. Boardman well to consult one of the many fortune tellers that set up shop along his Boardwalk – maybe she would have shed light on the strange fate he had in store. Almost at once, fortune tellers became as ubiquitous as salt water taffy and rolling chairs along the Atlantic City Boardwalk, and even today, settled snuggly between towers of temptation, where luck changes on the turn of a dime, clairvoyants are waiting to tell you your destiny.

A fortune teller's sign on the Boardwalk

One tidbit of Atlantic City ghostlore stems from these rather mysterious mainstays of the Boardwalk. But, like any folklore that has been passed down from less-enlightened times, sometimes traces of bygone prejudices and superstitions creep into the stories. Such is the case with a story unearthed from newspaper archives, which centers on a caricature of the dishonest old fortune teller.

On a weekend trip to Atlantic City, an Ocean County woman visited a Boardwalk palm reader, who, over the course of the reading, determined the presence of a hex on the woman. *One hundred dollars will remove the hex*, the fortune teller told her, *or*, noticing the woman's displeasure, *your wedding ring and bracelet would do.* In a huff of indignation, the woman left the shop, the fortune teller cackling after her, *I'll make that hex worse!*

A few nights later, the strange experience still flickering in the back of her mind, the woman woke in the middle of the night to the sweet, familiar smell of incense — the same scent that hung in the air of the

> In the 20th century, many Roma women (commonly known as Gypsies) became fortune tellers, honing their intuition and craft over generations. The pervasive skepticism about fortune tellers no doubt stems from the stereotypes against the Roma in general, which has led to a history of persecution. A very private and tight-knit people, many Roma families prefer to remain set apart from mainstream society in the U.S., hiding their heritage for fear of lingering prejudice.

fortune teller's shop in Atlantic City. No sooner did she make the connection then a figure of a man entered her bedroom, carrying a tray of burning incense. The entity soundlessly turned and walked away, its footsteps silent on the floors. Feeling something invisible tugging at her to get up, she stood and walked to the window. As her eyes adjusted to the blackness of the backyard, she saw two graves, side by side, newly dug in her yard. Strangely, although the graves were fresh, the headstones atop them were old and worn. To her horror, a high-pitched cackle suddenly echoed through the night — the exact eerie laugh of the fortune teller.

The next weekend, the woman returned to Atlantic City, this time armed with a hundred dollars and more jewelry. She headed straight for the palm

In Roma folklore, the vomit of an infectious ghost named "little grandmother," or *Mamorio*, is harvested from piles of trash and baked with flour. This "ghost vomit," or *coxai*, is said to be a powerful cure for illness. "Devil's dung," or *asafetida*, is another traditional Roma remedy. Funeral rites and grave markers also have an important place in Roma traditions. Final resting places are often decorated with elaborate lettering and urns, and sometimes fronted by paved areas with tables and chairs for family members to visit with their deceased loved ones.

reader. When she arrived at the shop, all that greeted her was a boarded up storefront. The fortune teller was gone. *They say she swindled customers*, explained the salt water taffy guy next door, *so the cops shut her down*. After that, no more graves appeared, no more ghosts or cackling old women awoke her in the middle of the night. Everything vanished, as if it were a dream.

The Ambassador Hotel's Shocking Séance

At first, the story seems made up, like the stuff of urban legend or pop culture myth. In 1922, famed magician Harry Houdini met up with renowned author Sir Arthur Conan Doyle for what began as a leisurely beachside vacation. It ended with a séance in the Ambassador Hotel that sent shockwaves through their friendship and supernatural circles around the world.

The Ambassador was built in 1919 as the largest hotel on the Boardwalk, with fourteen stories and four hundred rooms, and like many other grandiose resorts on the island, it ushered many of America's rich and famous through its doors, including senators from all over the country, President Warren Harding, and Enrico Caruso. But, as it was with many of the old-timers in Atlantic City, the elderly hotel just didn't have the look city officials were going for when they legalized gambling in 1976. Plans were put into motion to remodel to make way for the site of the new Tropicana Casino, but the city demanded the old Ambassador be leveled. Finally, a compromise was reached, where the structure would be taken down to its steel girders, giving the outside a total makeover. The result? The old bones of the Ambassador were entombed in the new brick façade of the Tropicana, as were the memories from the incredible events that took place that summer of 1922.

Sir Arthur Conan Doyle, the well-known author and creator of Sherlock Holmes, and his wife, Jean, were devout believers in Spiritualism, a belief system

Sir Arthur Conan Doyle embraced Spiritualism following a number of deaths in his family, including his first wife, Louisa, and their son, Kingsley. His belief in survival after death led him to join the well-known Ghost Club, based in London, which continues to research paranormal phenomena today. Doyle's beliefs in supernatural beings were not limited to ghosts; he also believed in, and published a book about, fairies.
Photo courtesy of Library of Congress

centered on life after death and communicating with the Other Side. Spiritualism got its start in the mid-nineteenth century with the famed Fox sisters of New York. The two women claimed to be in communication with ghosts through rapping noises. Rappings soon became a mediumistic mainstay, and from these rather obscure beginnings, Spiritualism became an international phenomenon, launching a surge of spirit circles, mediums, and séances, and counting among its ranks laypeople and celebrities alike. Doyle, in fact, was so devoted to the cult that he believed fate had impelled him to create a likeable and popular character in Sherlock Holmes, so that Doyle himself would be liked and popular. Once he gained his readers' confidence, he could then preach on behalf of Spiritualism.

Houdini, on the other hand, was a skeptic of all things supernatural. Being a magician, he knew the tricks of the trade, literally, and could easily decipher a sleight of hand or gimmick, which would later help his crusade against false mediums. Houdini was also a bibliophile and had a deep-seated love of high art; these two passions led to friendships with many

Houdini died on October 31, 1926, in the early morning hours of Halloween, from a ruptured appendix. In a morbid coincidence, Houdini's remains were delivered from Detroit to New York in the coffin he was supposed to use in an upcoming "buried alive" escape.

Houdini and his wife Bess made a pact that whoever died first would send the other a message known only to them. When Houdini died, Bess offered a $10,000 reward to anyone who could deliver to her the secret message from her husband. One medium, Arthur Ford, evidently tricked Bess by covertly obtaining the message. Bess later renounced any belief in life after death.

Photo courtesy of Library of Congress

famous writers, such as Edna Ferber, Edward A. Guest, Jack London, and, at the start of the 1920s, Sir Arthur Conan Doyle. Houdini himself was also a celebrity. Gaining fame throughout Europe as the "Handcuff King," he later met with huge success in the United States as an escapologist — escaping everything from crates, straitjackets, a whale, the infamous Milk Can, his Chinese Water Torture Cell, to a coffin.

Despite Houdini's hedging, Doyle was convinced that his friend was in possession of supernatural powers. How else, reasoned Doyle, could a man perform the feats Houdini did without the help of spirits? Doyle interpreted Houdini's denials as reluctance, and he used the Davenport brothers as justification for Houdini's attitude. The Davenports were magicians like Houdini, performing similar acts of superhuman escape. Unlike Houdini, however, the brothers were careful not to deny or to confirm any spirit interference. Instead, they left the interpretation of their performance to their audiences. Their ambivalence backfired, however, and they were persecuted for fourteen years, their lives and property destroyed by mobs. In Doyle's view, Houdini's renouncement of Spiritualism was merely self-preservation.

Still, they were friends — for a time. While on a lecture tour of the United States, the Doyles lodged for a time at the Ambassador Hotel in Atlantic City, inviting Houdini and his wife, Bess, for a visit the weekend of June 17th and 18th, 1922. One of the reasons Doyle had traveled to Atlantic City was to look into a large radio that boasted reception from Pittsburgh. At the time, 300 miles was an uncommon enough distance for radio waves to travel that he believed it might also be able to tune into the spirit world. He also hoped a visit with Houdini would finally convince the skeptic, or at least cause Houdini's powers to manifest. On the second day of their visit, Doyle approached the Houdinis as they sunbathed on the beach, suggesting he and Houdini go inside for an automatic-writing séance, at which Lady Doyle was proficient. Bess was not invited for fear of too much negative energy in the room.

Once inside the Ambassador, the séance began, with Lady Doyle as interlocutor of the spirit world. It turns out there was just one spirit seeking contact that day, Houdini's mother. People say there could not have been a more appropriate spirit to gain Houdini's confidence, for even Doyle once remarked that Houdini's devotion to his deceased mother was uncommonly passionate. In any case, Lady Doyle reluctantly offered to try to reach her through "inspired writing" and was almost immediately successful, furiously scribbling page after page, fifteen in all. From Lady Doyle's interpretation, for that's what automatic-writers do, the spirit of Houdini's mother was overjoyed at having finally made contact with her beloved son: "I am almost overwhelmed by this joy of talking to him once more," scrawled Lady Doyle, "...thank you, thank you, thank you, friend, with all my heart for what you have done for me this day — God bless you, too, Sir Arthur, for what you are doing for us — for us over here."

Doyle claimed that Houdini was deeply movcd

> Automatic writing was once a popular choice for psychic mediums attempting to communicate with the dead. Typically, a medium would enter a trance, whereby a spirit would begin to manipulate the medium's writing utensil, either pen on paper, chalk on slate board, or a typewriter. This method is not unlike using a planchette and an Ouija board, except it is quicker. Critics of automatic writing claim that the messages come from the writer's subconscious mind.

by the séance, even to the point of accepting it as true, yet others believe this was another of Doyle's misreadings of Houdini. Some time later, Houdini reflected on that afternoon in the Ambassador Hotel. First, he pointed out that Lady Doyle had scribbled a cross on the top of the page, which he felt would be inconsistent with his mother's Jewish faith. Doyle argued the cross is common for mediums to write. Second, Houdini attacked the fact that his mother's spirit seemed to be communicating in English when she never used it life. In response, Doyle argued that the use of English came from Lady Doyle, not Cecilia Weiss, since in automatic writing the medium is translating emotions and feelings, not words per se. Nevertheless, Houdini felt that even these translations did not seem like things his mother would express.

The third point of contention was Houdini's own casual, and very brief, attempt at automatic writing. After Lady Doyle had completed her trance, Houdini mused aloud whether he would be able to communicate with ghosts through writing. Picking up a pen, he wrote the word "Powell." If Doyle had needed more evidence that Houdini was psychic, that word was it. Apparently, a friend of Doyle's named

The two contradictory definitions of magic get at the heart of the complicated relationship between Doyle and Houdini:

1. The use of ritual activities or observances which are intended to influence the course of events or to manipulate the natural world, usually involving the use of an occult or secret body of knowledge; sorcery, witchcraft.

2. The art of producing (by sleight of hand, optical illusion, etc.) apparently inexplicable phenomena; conjuring. (*OED*)

Poster courtesy of Library of Congress

Ellis Powell had recently died, and Doyle believed his spirit visited them in their suite that day. Houdini, not surprisingly, balked at Doyle's insinuation, calling it coincidence and even a trick on Doyle's part. Still, Doyle felt the secret of Houdini's life was revealed: the magician was indeed in contact with the spirit world.

Houdini and Doyle's relationship never quite rebounded from their visit at the Ambassador Hotel, if it ever really got off the ground given their profound disagreements about Spiritualism. Doyle continued to insist on Houdini's psychic powers, writing a book, *The Edge of the Unknown*, and dedicating almost forty pages to a chapter titled "The Riddle of Houdini." Here, Doyle confides Houdini's supposed revelation of a psychic aspect to his performances, claiming that Houdini heard a voice inside his head that guided him through his onstage maneuvers. Not a move was made nor a step taken before he heard this disembodied voice. Doyle interpreted the voice as a spirit guide, something otherworldly that watched over Houdini. To hear the voice, of course, Houdini would have had to be a "sensitive," that is, receptive to the spirit world. Houdini merely scoffed at Doyle's interpretation of his intuition.

The séance attended by two of America's biggest twentieth century celebrities will always remain a mystery. Did Houdini's mother communicate with them that day? Did Doyle witness Houdini's powers manifest with the word "Powell"? Or was it all staged, contrived, and misinterpreted? If nothing else, does the complicated and emotionally charged energy from that day still echo through the renovated walls of the Tropicana Casino?

Tropicana Casino & Resort today

Ghosts and Gangsters

A rumrunner caught by the Coast Guard
Library of Congress

Only in Atlantic City could a decade like the Roaring Twenties be bookended with such iconic events. Opening with scenes from the netherworld featuring Houdini and Doyle's séance, Atlantic City's golden decade closed with a spectacle from the underworld, as powerful gangsters swept into the resort for an infamous meeting that would come to be known as the Atlantic City Conference.

The reason that the country's leading mob bosses chose the resort city was twofold. In the Prohibition era, Atlantic City hit pay dirt. Delivering the illicit activities denied most everywhere else, Atlantic City lived up to its reputation as the World's Playground. Alcohol, sex, and gambling establishments openly flourished – thanks to Nucky Johnson, Atlantic City's political boss who resolutely refused to deny people what they so obviously wanted. Organized crime leaders found this atmosphere an accommodating backdrop for their discussions about combining forces to maximize profits. Indeed, like Atlantic City, mobsters struck it rich during Prohibition, but, in 1929, they also had the foresight to plan for the inevitable resumption of legal alcohol manufacture and sale. This concern fell under Lucky Luciano's more pressing desire to take his multistate alliance ("The Seven Group," of which Nucky was a part) to the national level by way of a news wire that would facilitate gambling. Atlantic City, where illegal practices operated most openly, became a logical choice for a summit of people specializing in illegal practices. The second reason for choosing this location was also a logical one. It made for a nice honeymoon for New York mobster Meyer Lansky and Anna Citron.

With Nucky Johnson as their obliging host, gang leaders from Boston, Chicago, Cleveland, Detroit, Kansas City, northern New Jersey, New York, and Philadelphia arrived on the second weekend in May at the elite Breakers Hotel on the Boardwalk in Atlantic City. Unfortunately, things did not go as smoothly as they hoped. In an attempt to outsmart the WASPs-only policy at the Breakers, Nucky had made reservations for his multi-ethnic crew under false names. The management quickly caught on to the ruse when they saw Jewish and Italian men and women waiting for their rooms. Al Capone, Lucky Luciano, Meyer Lansky, and the rest were turned away, with seemingly little regard for their power and influence.

A quick phone call to Nucky remedied the situation, but not without another brief disruption. One of the most notorious bosses in history had been invited to the conference: the legendary Al Capone, believed by some to have been the most powerful man in the underworld at the time. Capone's racketeering prowess, honed under his "apprenticeship" with Chicago mobster Johnny Torrio, as well as his ruthlessly violent personality, led him to build a formidable empire in Chicago. In fact, just two months prior to the Atlantic City Conference, the infamous Saint Valentine's Day Massacre had erupted in Chicago, where seven men belonging to the "Bugs" Moran gang, Capone's rival, were gunned down execution-style by men dressed as police. It is widely believed that Capone ordered the killings, but lack of evidence prevented any charges. If you choose to believe the rumors, the Chicago massacre perhaps helps to explain what happened next in Atlantic City.

When Nucky arrived on the scene to fix the morass, the affronted mobsters were en route to the President Hotel, which was located between Hartford and Albany Avenues. Capone, volatile as ever, leapt out of his car and, in front of the entire entourage and other onlookers, began shouting at Nucky Johnson for his ineptitude. Even though Capone was on Nucky's turf, when they all finally arrived at the President Hotel, rumor has it that Capone continued his tirade – tearing things from the wall and throwing them around the lobby. The violent display seems a fitting, if not a little overdramatic, commencement to the initiation of a national mob syndicate.

The mobsters split themselves up between the President and the Ambassador Hotels (where Harry Houdini and Sir Arthur Conan Doyle had tried to summon Houdini's mother's spirit), while Meyer and Anna Lansky stayed at the Ritz-Carlton at Iowa Avenue and the Boardwalk. Their widely publicized meetings, covered by famed writer and journalist Damon Runyon, were reportedly held on the rooftops of the President and Ambassador. For the welcome parties, Nucky supplied every convenience and luxury imaginable, including fur coats for all the women in attendance, and women for all the solo men in attendance.

Each day after, legend has it, the gangsters would ride the rolling chairs to the end of the Boardwalk. They would remove their shoes (like any seasoned beachcomber), make their way through the sand, roll up the pant legs of their expensive suits, and walk into the water. There, only the seagulls could eavesdrop on their talk of illegal gambling, bootlegging, and other matters of risky business.

Some historians believe that one of the byproducts of the conference would be the abatement of what was seen as Capone's reactionary violence, as evidenced by the recent Saint Valentine's Day Massacre. However, the men in attendance at Atlantic City were not the only ones "concerned" about Capone. His death allegedly held a $100,000 reward, put forth by associates of the men killed in the Chicago massacre. For two months, people had been after Capone, even following him to Atlantic City and trailing him on the Boardwalk.

In some accounts, Capone made a pledge to a new era of peace after the conference. Indeed, this about-face is one reason given for his arrest in Philadelphia after leaving Atlantic City. It was the second time the fearsome Capone had ever been arrested; the first was a charge of Contempt of Court, for which he posted bond. After the conference, Capone and his bodyguard left by car for Philadelphia to catch a train back to Chicago. Their car broke down

> Three years after the Atlantic City Conference, notorious bootlegger Michael "Mickey" Duffy was murdered at the Ambassador Hotel, where the crime bosses stayed during the conference. Duffy's legacy of breweries extended from South Jersey to Camden to Philadelphia.

on the way, causing them to miss the train. While waiting for the next one, they caught a movie. On their way out of the theater, two Philadelphia cops approached them and asked them if they were carrying concealed weapons. Capone and his bodyguard gave up their guns, and they were taken in.

There are at least three theories as to what really happened. With such an easy arrest, some have speculated that everyone at the Atlantic City Conference had agreed that Capone would be their fall guy to distract the authorities for awhile. The cops were "friendly," and so were Capone's accommodations once he was incarcerated. Others heavily dispute that theory – would one of the most powerful bosses agree to be turned in to protect other gangs, regardless of the terms? – but still believe Capone arranged the arrest. His motivation lay in the $100,000 hit out on him. As he was being booked, he reportedly told the Public Safety Director of his troubles, claiming he was in constant fear of other racketeers and often had to conceal his identity, even to the point of registering under a fake name for the Atlantic City Conference. Others resist theories of collusion at all and stick to a simple storyline – that the incident happened without interference from either Capone or the men at the Atlantic City Conference.

Whatever may have precipitated the arrest, Capone faced a one year jail term, the maximum sentence for carrying concealed deadly weapons. Despite his best efforts to avoid the sentence (bribes and rewards), he was sent to the soon-to-be notorious Holmesburg prison in Philadelphia, Pennsylvania, until August of that year. At that point, he was transferred to Eastern State Penitentiary, in a different section of the city but equally notorious for its treatment of inmates, where, nowadays, curious tourists can view his eight-month cell.

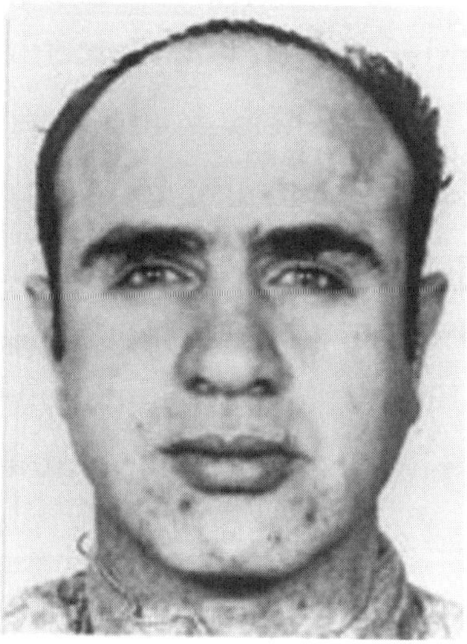

Al Capone's mug shot, 1939

A year and a half after his release from Eastern State Penitentiary, Capone received his biggest blow to date, an eleven year sentence in

Federal Prison, which he served at the U.S. Penitentiary in Atlanta, Georgia, and at the infamous Alcatraz Prison in California. If the Atlantic City Conference had been a turning point in Capone's life, as some biographers have theorized, then it certainly became a turn away from the lavish lifestyle he enjoyed previously.

After the Conference in Atlantic City, Capone's life seemed to spiral downward. To Capone's horror, the crime with which he was never charged was turning out to be his undoing. On more than one occasion, Capone confessed that the spirit of James Moran, one of the victims of the Saint Valentine's Day Massacre, had persistently haunted him. Sometime in 1931, Capone allegedly sought help from a medium due to the determination of the spirit to avenge his death. At both Eastern State Penitentiary and Alcatraz, inmates and guards recalled hearing the mob king cry out for "Jimmy" to leave him alone. By all accounts, Moran's spirit seemed to have attached

> To this day, people believe Al Capone's spirit returns to Alcatraz. Unexplainable banjo music has been heard coming from the shower area. During his incarceration there, Capone played the banjo in a band.

itself to Capone, preying on him like a leech.

Did the haunting of Capone first manifest here in Atlantic City, where he had the unmistakable feeling of being followed? Was his erratic behavior caused by the evidently terrifying and surely vengeful ghost of Jimmy Moran? Like other reported cases of spirit possession, Capone experienced severe behavioral changes, and his health declined. Sources say the ghost continued to haunt him until he died in 1947.

But there's another side to the story. At the same time Capone was suffering the taunts of Moran's ghost, his neurological system was steadily being eaten away by syphilis. Toward the end of his prison term, a doctor found him "poorly cooperative" and "viciously assaultive," with the cognitive level of an eighth grader. These were just a few of the symptoms of brain damage from untreated syphilis. Was the ghost of Jimmy Moran just in his mind after all?

> Many reported cases of possession involve a spirit with no apparent connection to the person possessed. Some believe entities seeking human hosts choose them at random, often based on proximity. Capone's alleged unwanted companion obviously strayed from standard practice.

The Phantom Darby Hicks

In the first few decades of the twentieth century, a mysterious person named Darby Hicks supposedly haunted the African-American community in Atlantic City with his phantom presence. Briefly mentioned in *The Guide to 1930s New Jersey* (1939), the author perhaps unintentionally stumbled upon a lost piece of Americana folklore, as further digging unearthed reports of this fabled man all over the country.

An 1899 report tells of a wild goose chase for a murdered man and one Darby Hicks in Birmingham, Alabama. The joke, as it turns out, was on the coroner and his two colleagues, for the tip was bogus and so was the murdered man. Hicks, they ambiguously say, was well-known about town. Another Darby Hicks made the news twenty years later in Louisiana, as a poetaster rhyming about footprints. And a 1909 notice records his visit to a Kansas hospital for a bullet in his kneecap. Evidently, Hicks briefly left his room after his wound was dressed. Upon his return, his curious explanation was that he had just been out for a stroll. The men involved in these incidents could have been using Darby Hicks as a pseudonym, or perhaps the stories are just part of a long tradition of Darby Hicks folklore. It's interesting to note, however, that over half of all recorded incidents of ghostly materializations involve apparitions not of the dead, as one might assume, but of the living.

Other incarnations of Darby Hicks side with the mythical. In World War II, he served a purpose similar to the iconic graffiti of "Kilroy was here," only he was the calling card of African-American troops. He haunts the line credits of Johnny Otis's albums as a phantom co-writer, taken, apparently, from the slang for a husband with an unfaithful wife. Similarly, he once haunted the minds and egos of rookie jazz musicians, who allegedly were always trying to keep up with the trickster Hicks, an amazing musician who would steal their girlfriends. He also takes the form of hipster Bob Washington's alter ego in his memoir, *Hip Recollections of Darby Hicks*.

As for Atlantic City's Darby Hicks, people would inform newcomers to the city that this Hicks fellow was in pursuit, and he was armed. The gullible initiate would then be sent from place to place on the trail of Hicks, with each stop bringing more terrifying threats. The cruel joke, it seems, was on the newbie, for legend has it he would go mad trying to track down his imaginary pursuer.

Resorts Hotel & Casino: A Portal to the Past

During World War II, between 1942 and 1946, Atlantic City was known as Camp Boardwalk. At night, all the windows facing the ocean were shuttered. Street lamps and neon signs remained unlit at dusk. Cars passing on nearby streets peered lazily into the night, with the top half of their headlights painted black. What looked like crude sand castles in the darkness turned out to be broken, battered ship parts washed ashore, and other beachcombers weren't pleasure-seekers at all, but armed, mounted members of the Coast Guard patrolling the beach for spies from German U-Boats lurking in the water. During the day, the Atlantic Ocean reflected an oily sheen. Gone were the familiar vacationers and honeymooners, and in their place were tens of thousands of soldiers, either training as new recruits or recovering as wounded veterans. They practiced their drills on the Boardwalk, used the hotels as their barracks, and performed mock invasions on the beach.

In addition to transforming into a basic training camp, Atlantic City also turned over many of its hotels for a hospital. By the end of 1943, nine hotels comprised the Thomas England General Hospital, as the medical complex was known. It became the largest amputee and neurosurgery hospital in the world.

Haddon Hall Hotel on the Boardwalk was the first hotel to be taken over for the hospital. At the time, it was paired with the Chalfonte Hotel, which stood across the street, and the two were known collectively as Chalfonte-Haddon Hall Hotel, the largest hotel by capacity in the city. From tee-totaling Quaker owners in its early years, to Merv Griffen, Donald Trump, and finally to Resorts International in the 1970s, when it became the first legal casino in the city, the property has had a colorful and storied life that remains evident in the typical modern casino front of the ground floor flanked by the grand architecture of the old Haddon Hall Hotel (the Chalfonte section was torn down for a parking lot). Today, the Haddon Hall section remains one of the few structures still standing from the resort's early days, and it is the site of frequent ghostly sightings and other strange occurrences.

A recent article suggests that many of today's paranormal experiences at Resorts are direct manifestations from the building's time as a hospital. In the dead of night, people have witnessed full apparitions of Army soldiers, some injured and infirm, in the hallways of the building and in the registration area on the first floor. The spirits' aloofness and unresponsiveness are often the only clues to their ghostly state.

In the elevators, people have reported hearing strange sounds unable to be attributed to any elevator mechanisms. It's possible that these suspected communications from the Other Side arise from an unsettling event that took place during the hospital years. In September 1944, a hurricane devastated the shore. Haddon Hall suffered the greatest injury, with five feet of water pouring into the cellar, severe damage to the physical therapy and artificial limb areas, and loss of power. Officials soon ordered the evacuation of patients, and it took nine hours to safely bring the recuperating soldiers to a waiting train. As the building slowly drowned, nurses carried many of the patients down eleven flights of dimly lit stairs. Some theorize that the sounds heard today in the elevator are really the phantom echoes of those soldiers hastily being ushered to safety.

> The legendary Peg Leg Bates visited Thomas England General Hospital in the 1940s, tap dancing his way through each ward in a five hour marathon performance. Born Clayton Bates in 1907, he lost his leg at age twelve, during the graveyard shift at a cotton mill. Already a dancing prodigy for seven years, his missing limb did not deter him, and he went on to become one of the most beloved entertainers of the 20th century. According to sources, his spirit can still be heard tapping down the Boardwalk in Atlantic City.

Every now and then, bystanders have witnessed a spectral scene appear out of thin air by the valet parking area. They say that ghostly nurses helping ailing children out of the building materialize before their eyes. The mirages come through the doors, out onto the sidewalk, and disappear. Some of the children walk feebly with a nurse on their arms; others are slowly pushed in old wheelchairs. Eyewitnesses who have glimpsed the faces of the children say they seem rather confused and sometimes mad. By all accounts, there were never any children admitted to the hospital.

Before World War II, Chalfonte-Haddon Hall was counted among the resort's premier honeymoon destinations. Perhaps that explains the spirits of a newlywed couple who gaze lovingly at each other as

> There is also word of a disheveled-looking fellow resembling Charlie Chaplin lurking in the shadows of the slot machines and gaming tables. This apparition is particularly interesting, and rather rare, as it appears to be what psychic researchers call a reciprocal apparition; that is, the spirit and witness seem to see each other, in this case, when the former nods its head hello. However, this type of encounter usually occurs between those who knew each other well in life, making these incidents with the vagrant ghost even more unusual.

they float through the hallways. Still enraptured with each other after all these years, the couple ignores all others around them, according to the same article. Of the more than 16 million people who fought in the U.S. armed forces in World War II, over 400,000 died. Some believe these sweetheart ghosts return to the scene of their happiest moments, before death did part them.

In the upper floors of the hotel, people have reported abnormally cold temperatures, often a sign of a supernatural presence. One guest reported feeling especially unnerved on the sixth floor, with the distinct feeling that she and her husband were not alone. After they turned the lights out to go to sleep, they both heard knocking sounds, the door knob rattling, and footsteps outside their door. When they (uneasily) investigated, they found the halls empty. Incidentally, a long time resident of Atlantic City remembers a number of soldiers committing suicide at the hotel/hospital, unable to come to terms with the loss of their limbs. Several of them took their own lives by jumping out the windows of the upper floors.

6th floor of Resorts Hotel & Casino, where disembodied footsteps have been heard

Steel Pier: Ghosts on my Mind

In the summer of 1952, Ronald Harrison climbed into a glass-topped, concrete grave he erected on Steel Pier and stayed there for six weeks, consuming only liquids and sleeping only four hours a night. While being buried alive may go down in history as one of the strangest economic protests (he was determined to "stay down 'til prices go down"), this morbid attraction was a spectator favorite, earning a place as one of the most memorable in Steel Pier's oeuvre of bizarre attractions. Many others were death-defying acts in their own right, including Atlantic City's infamous mascots, the High Diving Horses; the motorcycle madcap, CeDora; the high-wire adventurers, the Six Hustreis; the human cannon balls, the Flying Zachinis; and the boxing kangaroos and cats.

But the amusement pier at Virginia Avenue and the Boardwalk (now across from Trump Taj Mahal) wasn't all stunts and daredevils. In its glory years, Steel Pier, a.k.a. the Showplace of the Nation, also hosted the country's top entertainers, such as Charlie Chaplin, W.C. Fields, Bob Hope, Abbott and Costello, and, later, Frank Sinatra, Diana Ross, the Rolling Stones, Ray Charles, and many more.

The pier's long, vibrant life came to a close in 1982 — death by fire at the age of 84. At the time of the destructive blaze, it had been years since Steel Pier

Visitors in the 1890s excitedly lined up for a mystifying ride called the Haunted Swing, which stood on the Boardwalk at States Avenue, a couple of blocks up from Steel Pier. Passengers would climb aboard a platform that was surrounded by a fully furnished room, which would seem to spin upside down, defying gravity. In actuality, it was only the room that spun, but riders seemed none-the-wiser and clamored to experience the haunting sensation.

had been overrun with performers and visitors. Having weathered storms, a shipwreck, a previous fire, and years of neglect, it teetered above the water with one foot in the grave.

Around the same time as this catastrophic fire, sources say maintenance workers at the pier claimed that one of its famous performers had returned for a final performance. Although the millions who looked forward to the escapades at the Steel Pier had long since vanished, the legendary Louis Armstrong seemed to be playing his trumpet to the tune of "Georgia on my Mind." He hadn't performed there since the 1960s, and, more importantly, he was dead.

The fire left a small, 1,000 foot piece of the original Steel Pier, which was bought by Trump Taj Mahal in 1993. Since then, Trump replaced that piece with a sturdier concrete slab. With virtually every trace of the original Steel Pier gone, a modern day reincarnation rose in its place. It now operates as a

> The presence of Louis Armstrong's spirit was reportedly felt by a number of workers at Steel Pier, according to the newspaper article that reported the tale. This haunting would be what paranormal researchers call a collective incident, where more than one person experiences at the same time something they believe is supernatural.

family amusement park with rides and a midway jutting out over the beach and sea. Looking back at the experience of the workers in the rundown old pier, some believe that Armstrong's ghostly visit was an otherworldly omen of the second life in store for the legendary Steel Pier.

There's No Place Like Boardwalk Hall

Atlantic City ghostlore contains many accounts of ghostly hauntings that manifest in song. A common supernatural experience in general, discarnate songs are fitting considering the many entertainers who have passed through Atlantic City. An old newspaper article chronicles a number of these noisy ghosts: At Steel Pier, people hear Louis Armstrong's trumpet. Behind the Warner Theater façade at Bally's Casino, people listen to the faint strains of "Naughty Marietta"

sung by Jeannette MacDonald. Where the Globe Theater once stood at St. Charles Place and the Boardwalk, people hear Eddie "Banjo Eyes" Cantor crooning "Making Whoopie." But there's one tale of supernatural singing that stands out from the rest. It's set at the granddaddy of all Atlantic City venues, Boardwalk Hall, and it stars a woman widely regarded as one of the greatest female stars ever, Judy Garland. Years ago, people claimed they heard Garland's unmistakable voice singing during Ice Capades performances.

Taking up an entire city block on the Boardwalk between Mississippi and Georgia Avenues, Boardwalk Hall is an imposing stone structure fronted by Romanesque columns and a half-moon esplanade resembling an outdoor amphitheater. The colossal structure was built in 1929 with the intention of attracting conventions and their money-spending participants. It opened with much fanfare and with many claims to grandiosity. At the time, it was the largest building in the world standing without the help of roof posts or pillars. It housed the world's largest pipe organ with over 32,000 pipes, and it lodged the world's largest typewriter, a fourteen ton giant whose bell echoed down the block each time someone reached a new line on the nine by twelve foot paper. It also boasted the largest stage in the world, which was canopied by a reflective dome created by aluminum paint on sugar cane ceiling tiles. Interestingly, reflective surfaces have been linked to superstitions about death and ghosts since ancient times. In some folklore, people covered their mirrors and shiny surfaces for fear of seeing corpses or ghosts, either of which might carry away the unlucky onlooker's soul. Needless to say, Boardwalk Hall's magnificent ceiling would be a veritable graveyard of souls.

Boardwalk Hall, also known over time as Convention Hall and the Atlantic City Auditorium, has hosted nearly every imaginable incarnation of popular entertainment, from sporting events to circuses to star performances to the Miss America Pageant. Among the permanent fixtures was the Ice Capades, from

> Another superstition about mirrors and reflective surfaces holds that you should never look into one after dark or by candlelight. If you do, and you see a ghost or the devil, you will soon die. Mirrors are also believed to be dangerous for those in mourning, as they provide a way for ghosts of the newly departed to steal the souls of the living.

1941 through the 1980s.

Those who have heard Judy Garland's disembodied reprisal of "The Man That Got Away" might say her spirit chose a particularly poignant song with which to haunt the corridors of Boardwalk Hall. The song originally came from the soundtrack of her 1954 comeback movie, *A Star is Born*, but she continued to sing it on tour in the years to follow, including at Boardwalk Hall in 1961. The film itself follows the heartbreaking romance of a movie star couple whose fame leads to their undoing. Unable to handle his wife's success, the husband slowly drinks himself to humiliation. When he overhears his wife confide that she will abandon her career for him, he walks into the ocean and drowns himself.

One theory about hauntings in general suggests that the mysterious sounds, feelings, and touches we think of as paranormal activity are really imprints on another dimension called "psychic ether." When

Judy Garland's spirit is believed to frequent other venues as well. The Palace Theater in New York City, which claims over 100 ghosts, boasts recurrent sightings of an apparition resembling Garland at the entranceway at the rear of the orchestra pit, named after her and built specifically for her performances. She enjoyed one of her most renowned shows at the Palace Theater in 1951.

strong emotions accompany an event, these feelings can be imprinted onto this space and telepathically felt by sensitive people. Perhaps Garland's struggle with fame was strong enough to have imprinted this omnipresent field of psychic matter wherever she performed.

But another theory, which follows the more traditional thinking that hauntings are manifestations of spirits of the dead, takes a more empathetic approach to Garland's presence at Boardwalk Hall. If anyone in the industry felt the "other" side of fame, it was Judy Garland. Adored by millions, lavished with public praise, she struggled to her deathbed with celebrity's demons, including drug addiction and heartbreak. Could her haunting song be a cautionary tale meant for the many entertainers who perform the stage at Boardwalk Hall? Show business, she might argue, can be a lonely business.

Some theorize the song heard at Boardwalk Hall is not connected to Garland at all, but rather to a death right outside the building. In 1964, the Democratic National Convention met at Boardwalk Hall, where Lyndon B. Johnson was awarded the Democratic nominee for president. The convention was supposed to be a boon for the money-hungry city, as the 1960s were some of Atlantic City's darkest days with soaring crime and poverty rates and diminishing tourist dollars. Unfortunately, following the convention, the media spotlighted the negative feedback of the delegates, effectively burying Atlantic City as a "ghost town." To compound matters, on the last day of the convention, a woman jumped to her death, landing at the feet of the conventioneers. The news of the nearby suicide added a dark twist to the trenchant reports and, later, to the reason why the haunting melody of "The Man That Got Away" is heard in the vicinity.

Garden Pier:
One Last Dance

Toward the northern end of the Boardwalk, set slightly past the amusement piers, casinos, shops, and restaurants, sits Garden Pier, quietly welcoming the curious to its fantastic museum of Atlantic City relics and history. Never as famous as its cousins, Garden Pier nonetheless is one of the only extant "original" piers on the Boardwalk, and sources say it remains a favorite haunt of the long-departed "Latin Lover."

A silent film star of the 1920s, Rudolph Valentino made women across the world swoon in the theater aisles with his seductive moves and romantic roles. Some adored him, others envied him, but they were all enthralled by his smooth masculinity. Some say it was here, at Garden Pier, that he had a hunch that his magnetism would carry him far past the women who flocked to him for dance lessons. His fame following his big break as the lead in the film, *The Four Horsemen of the Apocalypse*, proved him right.

As "Valentino-mania" swept across the country, Valentino developed an avid interest in Spiritualism and the supernatural, in part through his association with June Mathis, who casted him in his breakthrough role. Valentino had a self-professed sensitivity to the unseen world, and Mathis' mother, once she passed away, often communicated with Valentino. He channeled his mediumistic powers through automatic writing (like Lady Doyle), and his book, *Day Dreams* (1921), contains pages and pages of poems he received from the Other Side, according to his second wife, Natacha Rambova, who shared her husband's interest in the paranormal.

In death, Valentino's spirit is believed to have made frequent contact with the living. In addition to treasured "visits" to Rambova, a British psychic named Leslie Flint claimed in the mid-1900s to have channeled Valentino's spirit through his unique method of Independent Direct Voice. This technique enabled participants to engage in full conversations with those who had passed away, but the conditions required a room of total darkness so visual manifestations were not common. The voice of the deceased would emanate from a space above Flint's head, he said, independent of him. In some instances, if the energy was strong enough, an ectoplasmic voice box would form in the air, which acted as a microphone, projecting the voices into the room. At the height of Flint's popularity, people flocked to experience his special gift, hoping perhaps to hear the voices of their loved ones or of the famous. Valentino was the first spirit to make contact through him, which given Flint's background seems rather fitting. At a young age, Flint remembered hearing ghostly chatter at theaters showing only silent films, and, at various times in his life, he was a ballroom dancing teacher and a theater usher.

Rudolph Valentino
Library of Congress

Flint and Valentino also played roles in an unusual work titled *The Voice of Valentino* (1965), by Lynn Russell, which chronicles Russell's spiritual journey to communicate with the spirit of "Rudy." Virtually unaware of the film star at the start of her psychic exploits, she comes to understand that she is tied to him across the divide of earthly and spirit realms, having been his sister in previous lives. After over eight years of séances, many with the help of Leslie Flint's Independent Direct Voice, she and her spirit circle become inspired by Valentino's message of love, his explanation of reincarnation, and his revelation of a divine plan involving the formation of a society devoted to the Other Side.

Today, Valentino continues his interest in the supernatural, but his spirit seems to prefer moonlit trysts to séances, at least in Atlantic City. In the shadows at the end of Garden Pier, where a ballroom once stood, people claim a ghostly apparition appears, twirling one partner after another in a romantic, deathly dance. The handsome profile and the graceful gait, they say, are unmistakably those of the dashing Valentino. He and his faceless partners perform this ethereal cotillion to a symphony of ocean waves, oblivious to any earthly audience.

Valentino met an untimely death in 1926 at the age of 31, due to a post-surgical infection. 100,000 mourners reportedly flocked to the funeral home in New York City, and another 80,000 met his casket in Los Angeles when his body was transported west for burial. The nation mourned, but perhaps no one more so than the mysterious "Lady in Black" who visited his mausoleum every year on the anniversary of his death, clad in black mourning clothes and carrying roses. The mystery woman revealed twenty years later that she and Valentino had made a pact when she was a young girl on her death bed. Valentino promised her she would outlive him, and when she did, she must visit his grave to talk to him. She recovered after he died and fulfilled her promise. Strangely, many other women then came forward, each claiming that she was the original "Lady in Black." The tradition continues to this day.

Lady Luck Defeated

Atlantic City's first jail, built in 1856 at Atlantic and Vermont Avenues
Absegami: Annals of Eyren Haven & Atlantic City

Firsthand encounters with spirit activity can be fragmented and unfinished. A movement out of the corner of your eye, a drop in the room temperature for no reason, or footsteps where no one treads. The experiences, like ghosts themselves, are frequently hazy and indistinct. A good example comes from my grandmother, whose family lived near California and Arctic Avenues in the 1930s. Whenever her uncles were in the attic, they would hear people behind them. They would turn, but of course they always found themselves alone. They didn't tell anyone about their experiences, not even each other, until many years later. Another cold case pops up at a mansion on Raleigh Avenue, near the beach, that scared all of the neighborhood kids with eerie encounters that couldn't easily be explained away. Same with an abandoned Spanish villa in west Atlantic City, once used by rumrunners. People would whisper about the strange-goings on there, which were always attributed to a vengeful poltergeist who was angered by the decorative installation of a sacred Mexican altar.

Sometimes, the best way to try to get to the bottom of a haunting is to poke in the dark corners of a town's discarded and forgotten tales. Sometimes, you wish you hadn't.

The very first murder on the island involved a politician from Philadelphia named Thomas Shriner who, on the day he drew his very last breath, was at the construction site of his new business venture. Prospects were high in the new resort, and he was in the process of building a hotel at the corner of Atlantic and Kentucky Avenues. According to Heston, a carpenter at the site fatally stabbed Shriner in the side with his compass. Whatever may have passed between the two men to occasion such an insubordinate reaction remains unknown, but the nameless carpenter claimed it was all in self-defense. Without anyone to challenge his version of the story, the carpenter walked. Shriner went to the grave without retribution for his ill-timed departure from this world.

Vengeance, by turns both heartless and passionate, played out in a ghastly murder that took place on New Year's Eve in the late 1800s on the beach to the north of Atlantic City. While all of the residents of the resort celebrated at the local Methodist Church, two lives were cut brutally short.

That night, the lullaby of ocean waves was shattered by the commotion of young Jesse Gandy as he swung an ax through the head of Daniel Turner, whose sister Eliza had rebuffed Jesse's flirtations. The turmoil escalated. Eliza quickly wrestled the ax from Jesse, threw it and a nearby gun outside, scooped up her dying brother, and carried him upstairs. Injured by a gunshot to her arm, but not ready to surrender, she flung herself out the window and fled to the neighbor's house. Jesse retaliated by burning the house down. The flames stunned witnesses in Atlantic City, who had finished their New Year's celebration but were too far away to prevent the tragedy. Daniel and the neighbor's daughter, Georgia Smith, who was staying at the house, perished in the fire.

No one can know what Jesse Gandy felt as he watched the house burn. Did he hear the screams for help and try to rescue Daniel and Georgia? Did he laugh, cry, or stand in disbelief at the nightmare unfolding before him that he himself brought to life? The only thing we do know is that at some point in the early hours of the first day of the New Year, Jesse crawled into his boat, pushed off into the bay, positioned his rifle so that he could pull the trigger with his foot, and shot himself in the head. The focus of his errant affection, Eliza, went on to marry Georgia's father, Mark, to whom she ran for help that awful night.

Years later, Bernard W. Lewis, a Pittsburgh man wracked either by remorse or by fear, shot himself in his bathroom at the States Villa, an upscale

An ancient Assyrian superstition tells of the evil spirit *ekimmu*, which can parasitically attach itself to someone living, causing a number of disturbances ranging from paranormal antics to the deaths of the person's family. A ghost can become an *ekimmu* by, among other things, dying violently or by having an unburied corpse.

guest house once located on South States Avenue, behind where the Showboat Casino now stands. His saga made national headlines when he was implicated in the murder of Mazie Colbert, an advertising model who was killed in Philadelphia, PA. He took his own life while the police were en route to arrest him. Afterward, a suicide letter turned up that was penned twelve days before Colbert's slaying. Three months later, a jury decided there was not enough evidence to convict Lewis (had he been alive), and Colbert's murderer remained at large.

On the other side of the island, a crime of passion continues to haunt the marshes between Atlantic City and the mainland. Long ago, a young man went to the gallows, which in those days was a

The legend of the disembodied "screaming skull," which dates back to at least the sixteenth century, warns of the consequences of not following someone's burial wishes. Victims of violent deaths whose deathbed wishes aren't respected will return to haunt the home in which they wish to be buried. The "screaming" takes the form of odd noises and poltergeist activity that become such a nuisance to the inhabitants of the house that they disinter the skull and place it prominently in the house. The ghost stays content until someone tries to remove the skull from the home, in which case the ghost retaliates with vengeance, cursing the people with bad luck or death, or destroying the home and its land.

public spectacle where the accused was strung up by a noose on the limb of a tree, for the gruesome murder of his beloved. As legend tells it, jealousy worsened by too many drinks caused this man to chop off his girlfriend's head with a butcher's saw. Ever since, the woman's headless spirit can be seen roaming the wetlands at midnight, her severed head tucked snugly between her arm and torso. Witnesses of the grisly apparition claim they have seen in the distance an equally disturbing phantom scene: the spirit of her boyfriend, neck cocked, arms and legs slack, dangling like a piece of rotted fruit.

History has a strange way of echoing itself, a phenomenon that sometimes stems from residual spirit energy, especially when intense emotions and unnatural deaths are involved. This residual energy perhaps explains people's reactions when they walk into a house, a building, or a park where a murder took place. At times, the energy lingers in the air like humidity on a hot summer day. Its presence isn't visible, but you can feel it on your skin.

Such lingering auras might be the case with an infamous murder of the 1980s, which began to unravel when a woman's bones were found in the marshes along one of the roads connecting the island to the mainland, perhaps the same place the headless ghost appears. The crime is just one piece of an odd puzzle involving one of Atlantic City's most famous families, who seemed unable to shake a curse of misfortune and tragedy.

The story begins back in the 1940s. If there was one place that represented the atmosphere of Atlantic City then and in the next two decades, it was the 500 Club. Steeped in hipness with a little bit of danger lurking around the edges, the 500 Club was a microcosm of the entire city. On any given night, you might have spotted glamorous Elizabeth Taylor at the winding bar that was decked out with a waterfall, or maybe Joe DiMaggio at his private table backdropped by zebra-skin wallpaper. Philly's "Gentle Don," Angelo Bruno, may have stepped out of the

Frank Sinatra

phone booth that led to a secret, elite gambling room, and any number of New Jersey's political bigwigs could have been enjoying the bottles of booze set at each individual table. On one of the stages, you might have been lucky enough to witness Dean Martin and Jerry Lewis perform their very first comedic duet together. And, if you could see through the throngs of people, you also could have been entertained by Frank Sinatra, who began performing here in 1957 and returned every year.

The 500 Club owed its iconic popularity solely to Skinny D'Amato, a legend in Atlantic City for his cool character, his famous friends (Frank Sinatra was one of his best), his ambiguous relationship to organized crime, and his charity. At one point, he was even crowned "Mr. Atlantic City" for his benevolence, which included anonymously paying medical bills, supplying coal and food, hosting fundraisers, and more goodwill for which he wanted no recognition.

Things began to change in 1972, when Bettyjane D'Amato, Skinny's wife of twenty-three years, died of a burst brain aneurysm. A year later, someone at the 500 Club accidently threw a lit cigarette into a trashcan that sat next to the bar's stock of matchbooks. Climbing up the curtains of the dressing room, the flames swiftly ate through the club and the restaurant (named Angelo's, after Skinny's son) behind it, leaving a heavy, black blanket in its wake. The fire charred everything except one thing. Above one of the burned-out stages, a huge portrait of Frank Sinatra gazed at the ruins. It had survived unscathed by fire or by water. Through his tears, Skinny called it a miracle.

But the darkness had already descended, and, before it lifted again, three more people would be dead. Three years after the 500 Club burned down, Skinny's son Angelo bludgeoned his friend to death in the basement of the D'Amato home. In later interviews with author Jonathan Van Meter, Angelo insisted he killed his friend because the latter had made passes at him, but speculation points to a deeper psychological rift as the motive, namely Angelo's feelings of inadequacy in the eyes of his father. He also blamed the destruction of the 500 Club, claiming that if it had never burned down, he would have never crossed paths with the victim, whom he met through his next job. Any compulsory reflection, however, was short-lived. Angelo's lawyers, whom Skinny hired, engineered a plea bargain that caused a sensation. After serving 33 months of a 10 year sentence, he was released. Rumors abounded that longtime family friend, Frank Sinatra, had bought Angelo's freedom.

Count: two dead, two to go.

Less than a year and a half after his release from prison, Angelo got into trouble again. At the end of 1980, he befriended a couple who moved in the shadier circles of Atlantic City. The man was a drug addict, his girlfriend a high-end prostitute. A few months after they began hanging out, the man discovered Angelo and the woman were romantically involved. A blow-out ensued. The woman disappeared the next day.

Frank Sinatra's spirit is believed to haunt the main showroom of the infamous Cal-Neva Lodge, which sits directly atop the California and Nevada border at Lake Tahoe, a cursed business venture in which he, Skinny D'Amato, Dean Martin, and others invested, in one way or another, beginning in 1960. A spectral presence in Chalet 52 has been attributed to Marilyn Monroe, who stayed there in the weeks before she died. She and Sinatra were rumored to have been romantically involved during Sinatra's ownership of the resort. Joe DiMaggio, Monroe's inconsolable ex-husband, evidently blamed Sinatra, the Kennedys, and Skinny D'Amato for her death.

At the same time, Angelo had begun embezzling money from the construction company for which he worked, and by April 1981, he again was sent to jail. Later that year, a bout of bragging in prison implicated him in the murder of the missing woman. But it wasn't until a fisherman discovered some of her remains in an Atlantic City marsh that authorities were able to advance their case against Angelo. The story the cops decided to believe was the boyfriend's — that Angelo had strangled the woman over $100 and dismembered her, and the two men then disposed of her remains in various places throughout the city. That is, all except for her severed head, which, according to Van Meter's research, Angelo concealed in his father's garage.

The next year, Angelo returned to prison, this time with a twenty-seven-year sentence. His beleaguered father (and Sinatra, for that matter) remained silent.

There was just one more tragedy to befall this weary family. One year after Angelo's incarceration, Skinny D'Amato's weak heart gave out. He died in the Frank Sinatra wing of the Atlantic City Medical Center. The curse, it seems, died with him.

Where There is a Sea, There are Pirates

Absecon Island's history of bandits and villains extends well into its past. For example, in the lingo of yesteryear, the term "wrecker" could have meant one of two things: a person who helps the shipwrecked, or a person who causes a shipwreck. The line between the two wasn't always distinct, but the latter type often leaned less toward the helpful side and more to the premeditated piracy side. The reputation of this type of wrecker — also sometimes referred to as a mooncusser — was notorious up and down the east coast from at least the eighteenth century, and ship crews the world over feared falling into one of their nefarious traps.

Mooncussers in particular gained infamy for

> Although the bobbing lights that lured ships to their wrecking were always attributed to mooncussers, the lights' characteristics bear an eerie similarity to the death omens known variously throughout the world as corpse candles, corpse lights, or ghost lights. Legend has it these lights appear at night like flames of a candle floating in the air. Some believe they point to the witness' gravesite, and sometimes an ethereal funeral procession is seen with them.

their cruel ploys designed to lure ships close enough to shore to cause them to run aground. They used many tactics, one of which was to hang a lantern around a donkey's neck and lead it back and forth. To a captain out at sea, the bobbing light looked like a fellow vessel. These false assurances would often lead the captain to venture closer to the shore until ramming his ship into the rocky embankment hiding in the water's shallow depths.

It was just such a crafty maneuver that spawned another ghost story associated with Brigantine's beaches, according to a well-known legend. Over the years, eyewitness accounts of a female apparition that appears on the shore formed into a juicy bit of Brigantine folklore. Although many details of the mournful tale associated with this spirit are lost to history, even the short version of the story remains fraught with double-crossing, betrayal, and heartbreak. Legend has it that this spirit roams the beach in search of her fiancé, who lost his life when his ship wrecked on the Brigantine shoals. But that's not even the most tragic part of the story. The reason the ship did not stay far enough to sea?

Edward Teach, a.k.a. Blackbeard
1736 engraving by J. Basire

sea? A mooncusser's ruse to lure it closer. The mooncusser? The woman's father. It is not known whether the woman ever married, whether she ever forgave her father, or whether she died from heartbreak, but once she departed from this life, her spirit returned to the site of her fiancé's demise, hoping, perhaps, to meet him again in the afterlife.

But of all the lore of the sea, perhaps none is as simultaneously heartless and enthralling than the legends of pirates. Two of the most notorious figures of the pirate trade — Blackbeard and Captain Kidd, whose names are virtually synonymous with piracy — have ties to the Jersey shore and to the waters north of Atlantic City in particular. As the stories go, these two buccaneers stole away in the thickets beyond Brigantine Inlet and Little Egg Harbor, leaving behind haunting tales of buried treasure and a few discarded bodies of disloyal shipmates.

One time while Blackbeard pirated in the Caribbean, he caught word that the authorities were in pursuit of him. He fled to the Jersey coast, sailing into Little Egg Harbor and hiding on an island behind Brigantine. When the British arrived to search for him, he hid underwater, breathing through a small reed until the search party left.

Blackbeard's well-known visit here is less a testament to his ruthlessness as it is to his cunning. Legends passed down for centuries have given him the reputation for being the most coldblooded pirate, even going so far as making a man eat his own ears and nose before he was killed. The nickname Blackbeard came from his startling black beard, which he would twist up in ribbons to add to his terrifying look. To look even more intimidating, he would also stick slow-burning matches into his braided hair when he attacked ships.

Another story tied to the Jersey shore relishes the romantic side of piracy. Some narratives of Captain Kidd's controversial life story say that he fell in love with a woman named Amanda from Ocean County, and she persuaded him to abandon his pirating career and settle down in South Jersey. Before he joined her, however, he divided the loot he

An ancient legend tells of a pirate whose soul was carried off to the afterworld by the Ship of the Dead when the mythical ship passed over the pirate's earthly home, enveloping the house with sounds of lightning and thunderclaps.

18th century portrait of Captain Kidd

A popular 19th century song about Kidd characterized him more generously than the legends did: "My name was Captain Kid, Farewell to young and old, All jolly seamen bold; You're welcome to my gold, For I must die, I must die."

had between his crew members and buried the rest at Brigantine. Kidd and Amanda took the whereabouts of this treasure to their graves, and it has never been found, although not for lack of trying.

And still other tales of pirates turn toward the supernatural. One day over 300 years ago, Captain Kidd anchored off the coast of Brigantine, seeking a hiding spot for his treasure. Venturing ashore with his First Mate, Timothy Jones, and other crew, Kidd found a suitable spot within some dunes. When the sea chest was buried, Kidd sent the crew back to the ship, holding Jones back from the rest. He and an unsuspecting Jones then relocated the riches. At that point, and no one knows the reason, Kidd and Jones squared off in a heated argument. Captain Kidd returned to his ship alone and sailed away.

Timothy Jones was buried in the ground with the loot, so that his ghost could guard it from future

Across many cultures, candles have long been associated with death, funereal rites, and the afterlife. Some customs call for burning candles to encircle a corpse until it is buried as a way of fending off demons and evil spirits. In the U.S., some believe an unattended burning candle portends a death in the family. At least since the 1600s in certain European cultures, a dim or blue flame indicates an unseen presence nearby.

treasure hunters. Folklore passed down from the seventeenth century advised people on the search for buried treasure to carry consecrated candles in lanterns, which were believed to wake up the dead sentries, like Timothy Jones, from their slumber beneath the earth. If the ghosts were able to unburden themselves of the treasure's location, they could then forsake their posts and finally rest in piece. There was, of course, a catch. The treasure seeker could not scream or gasp or make any noise whatsoever when faced with one of these ghastly spirits, or else the treasure would disappear forever.

Between the Devil and the Deep Blue Sea

Woodland path through the Pine Barrens,
the roaming grounds of the Jersey Devil
Absegami: Annals of Eyren Haven & Atlantic City

Around the same time that Captain Kidd and Blackbeard were raising hell up and down the Jersey coast, an overworked and bitter mother of twelve wearily braced herself to give birth to her thirteenth child in her home at Leeds Point, a small, desolate track of land to the north of Atlantic City. *Let it be a devil!*, she cursed, as a nor'easter pummeled the house, as if corralling a morass of evil energy to fulfill the broken woman's wish. The few women tending to her birth peered tensely at Mrs. Leeds' newborn, and uttered a small, collective sigh of nervous relief when the baby appeared to be a normal, healthy boy, for hadn't there been rumors that Mrs. Leeds dabbled in black magic?

The old women hardly had time to exchange the briefest of looks when the flawless baby suddenly metamorphosized before their eyes. Ten toes transformed into two inhuman hooves, and a long, forked tail sprouted before their eyes...this baby was indeed cursed. The sweet, round face elongated to that of a horse's, from the once-tiny shoulders extended wings like those of a monstrous bat, and soon the unearthly creature towered over the terrified women, including his mother. With a piercing cry of his own, the devil child bounded from the stunned covey, his tail whipping about with surly abandon, and flew out the window into the violent storm. The Jersey Devil was born.

Well, that's one version of the story. The legend exists in various forms with different details. Instead of a storm, there was fog. A preacher or a gypsy cursed the baby, not Mother Leeds, and when the baby was born, he sprouted leathery wings and grew to the size of a goat, resembling a cross between a bat and a kangaroo, and then killed his parents when he was four years old.

People have long sought natural explanations for the existence of the Jersey Devil. One theory posits that the creature is really a Sand Hill Crane, a native Jersey bird that boasts a wingspan of eighty inches and stands four feet high. The crane possesses a violent temperament when provoked, a bellowing call, and a propensity for farm crops and chicken eggs, much like the Jersey Devil. Another theory proposes

The Jersey Devil legend has striking similarities to an old world superstition about a young woman giving birth to a monstrous infant resembling the devil. Research conducted in Chicago, Illinois, in the early 1900s surrounding the phenomenon of a supposed resident "Devil Baby" found numerous versions of the legend in nearby Italian, Irish, and Jewish communities. The aberration came to pass in different ways according to the different ethnicities, but all included some perceived deviance on the part of the pregnant woman, and some included a spoken curse before the birth.

that the Jersey Devil was really a deformed child, whom Mother Leeds kept prisoner in her house. Her death (from natural causes) necessitated his escape, but rather than seek help from a neighbor, he secluded himself deep in the Pine Barrens.

People have also put forth unnatural explanations for the existence of the Jersey Devil, most commonly that the creature is the Devil incarnate or a demon underling. Some versions of the Jersey Devil legend say that Mother Leeds practiced witchcraft, and, interestingly, the legend sprung up just a few decades after the centuries-long spate of witch hunts in England and North America. Since the Middle Ages, Christians believed women accused of witchcraft had sex with demons, or, more explicitly, that demons could masquerade as humans and have sex with mortals, producing grotesque, fearsome offspring.

Although they say the devil is in the details, this is one tale that always has the same outcome. Whatever was born that night took up residence in the Pine Barrens, and for over 300 years, he would venture out every so often to the amazement and horror of the unlucky witnesses. And while the Jersey

Left: A drawing of the Jersey Devil from 1909, the year of Phenomenal Week
Philadelphia Post

Right: Chalkie Leeds, Atlantic City's first mayor
Absegami: Annals of Eyren Haven & Atlantic City

Some say Mother Leeds, the woman left in the wake of the Jersey Devil myth, was the first Leeds woman to travel from England to the New World. Years later, her descendents would be the first year-round residents of what would become Atlantic City. Is it any wonder that Atlantic City should have such a devil-may-care attitude?

Devil wouldn't be considered a ghost by modern standards, there are those who would swear up and down that he still haunts this area.

The number of sightings of the Jersey Devil could make even the most hardened nonbeliever into a devil's advocate, so to speak. Two of the earliest recorded experiences come from rather surprising sources. Both Commodore Stephen Decatur, of Revolutionary War and War of 1812 fame, and Joseph Bonaparte, King of Spain and brother to Napoleon, had violent run-ins with the Devil in the first decades of the nineteenth century. Scattered reports came in throughout the next 100 years from Haddonfield, Brigantine, Leeds Point, and more. But by 1903, folklorist Charles Skinner announced the metaphorical death of the Jersey Devil due to lack of interest and incidents.

Then, in 1905, the head lightkeeper of Absecon Lighthouse in Atlantic City, Thomas Bills, reported seeing him at the top of the lighthouse tower. Four years later, what had been considered a mere superstition by many, turned into an astonishing and frightening reality. Over the course of January 16th to January 23rd, 1909 – a week appropriately dubbed

Phenomenal Week — the Jersey Devil reawakened. And it seemed he was out for blood.

From as far west as the suburbs of Philadelphia County, north to Middlesex County, and east to Atlantic County in New Jersey, reports of the Jersey Devil's shenanigans quickly and repeatedly surfaced. Shocking and vivid firsthand accounts ran as front page news in many area newspapers, as did the efforts at vigilante justice and the concerned cautions of the authorities. Over one thousand people reported seeing the winged monster. Schools closed, neighbors locked their doors, and businesses remained dark.

With every horrifying incident came a renewed fervor to kill the strange creature, and weapons of every kind were employed, from brooms to stones to bullets. One of only two reported injuries to the Jersey Devil during this week comes from an Atlantic City man, who told his astounding story to a reporter:

> In an isolated spot in the Jersey Pines...I raised my gun and fired. One shot broke a wing and it fell to the ground, uttering hideous screams; but before anyone could collect his wits the thing was up

> and off with long strides and a sort of hop, dragging one wing, and then disappearing into the pine thicket.

Time and again, the Jersey Devil managed to escape death to retreat to his secret den in the Pine Barrens — hunted, lonely, and forsaken.

Evidence of the Jersey Devil's furtive existence continued throughout the twentieth century, albeit nothing like the events of Phenomenal Week. Every now and then, an incident would be blamed on him — such as the Invasion of Gibbsboro in 1951, when animal attacks, footprints, sightings, and screams were attributed to the legendary creature — and he would briefly capture the public's imagination again. At the same time, reports of his death would also emerge, all of which would prove to be hoaxes.

Is the Jersey Devil real? Or is he a projection of the same fears and fascinations that give us vampires, werewolves, and other creatures of the night? Many believe he does exist, but perhaps these aren't even the right questions. Maybe a more appropriate question would be this: If you were driving along the Atlantic City Expressway one quiet, moonless night, and unexpected car problems caused you to pull over on the side of the road, and you looked out your window into the thick, impenetrable woods of the Pine Barrens, would you be scared?

Bibliography & Acknowledgments

Boucher, Jack E. *Absegami Yesteryear*. Somers Point: Atlantic County Historical Society, 1963.

Capo, Fran. *It Happened in New Jersey*. Guilford: The Globe Pequot Press, 2004.

D'Amato, Grace Anselmo. *Chance of a Lifetime: Nucky Johnson, Skinny D'Amato and How Atlantic City Became the Naughty Queen of Resorts*. Harvey Cedars: Down the Shore Publishing, 2001.

Donio, Greg. "Grave Mutations: A Collection of South Jersey Ghost Stories." *Press of Atlantic City*.

—. "South Jersey's Haunts are a Grave Matter." *Sunday Press*. 25 October 1981.

Doyle, Sir Arthur Conan. *The Edge of the Unknown*. New York: G.P. Putnam's Sons, 1930.

Guiley, Rosemary Ellen. *The Encyclopedia of Ghosts and Spirits*. 2nd ed. New York: Checkmark Books, 2000.

Hearn, Lafcadio. *Kwaidan: Stories and Studies of Strange Things*. Boston: Houghton Mifflin & Co, 1904.

Heston, Alfred M. *Absegami: Annals of Eryen Haven and Atlantic City 1609 to 1904*. Vol 3. Atlantic City: Alfred M. Heston, 1904.

Johnson, Nelson. *Boardwalk Empire: The Birth, High Times, and Corruption of Atlantic City*. Medford: Plexus Publishing, 2002.

Kobler, John. *Capone: The Life and World of Al Capone.* New York: De Capo Press, 1971.

Legato, Frank. *Atlantic City, In Living Color*. Macon: Indigo Custom Publishing, 2005.

Levi, Vicki Gold and Lee Eisenberg. *Atlantic City: 125 Years of Ocean Madness*. 2nd ed. Berkeley: Ten Speed Press, 1979.

Lipsitz, George. "Songs of the Unsung: The Darby Hicks History of Jazz." *Uptown Conversations: The New Jazz Studies*. Ed. Robert G. O'Meally et al. New York: Columbia U Press, 2004.

McCloy, James F. and Ray Miller, Jr. *The Jersey Devil.* Wilmington: Middle Atlantic Press, 1976.

McMahon, William. *The History of Lucy: The World's Largest Elephant*. Margate: The Save Lucy Committee, 1988.

—. *Pine Barrens Legends & Lore*. Moorestown: Middle Atlantic Press, 1980.

—. *So Young...So Gay! The Story of the Boardwalk, 1870-1970*. Atlantic City: Atlantic City Press, 1970.

McPhee, John. *The Pine Barrens*. New York: Farrar, Straus and Giroux, 1967.

Mischlich, Marston A. "Atlantic City Answers the Call to World War II." Marston A. Mischlich, 1998. <http://venus.atlantic.edu/amatol/thesis_home.html>

Nash, Jay Robert. *World Encyclopedia of Organized Crime*. New York: De Capo Press, 1993.

Nelson, William. *The New Jersey Coast in Three Centuries*. New York: Lewis Publishing Co, 1902.

New Jersey: A Guide to its Present and Past. Compiled and written by the Federal Writers' Project of the Works Progress Administration for the State of New Jersey. American Guide Series. 1939.

Reeser, Tim. *Ghost Stories of Ocean City, NJ*. Monocacy: 1stSight Press, 2003.

Roberts, Russell and Rich Youmans. *Down the Jersey Shore*. New Brunswick: Rutgers U Press, 1993.

Schill, Brian. "The Devil Endures." *Haunted Times*. 4:2 Fall 2009.

Scoblete, Frank. "The Ghosts of Atlantic City's Resorts Hotel." *Casino City Times*. 25 February 2010 <http://scoblete.casinocitytimes.com/ article/the-ghosts-of-atlantic-citys-resorts-hotel-57722>

Silverman, Kenneth. *Houdini!!! The Career of Erich Weiss*. New York: HarperCollins, 1996.

Sloat, Warren. *1929: America Before the Crash*. New York: Cooper Square Press, 2004.

Sokolic, William H. and Robert E. Ruffolo Jr. *Atlantic City Revisited*. Images of America Series. Charleston: Arcadia Publishing, 2006.

Stanfield, Charles A. *Haunted Jersey Shore: Ghosts and Strange Phenomena from the Garden State Coast*. Mechanicsburg: Stackpole Books, 2006.

Tales of New Jersey. New Jersey Bell Telephone Co, 1963.

Van Meter, Jonathan. *The Last Good Time: Skinny D'Amato, the Notorious 500 Club, and the Rise and Fall of Atlantic City*. NY: Crown Publishers, 2003.

Veit, Richard F. and Mark Nonestied. *New Jersey Cemeteries and Tombstones: History in the Landscape*. New Brunswick: Rutgers U Press, 2008.

Waltzer, Jim and Tom Wilk. *Tales of South Jersey: Profiles and Personalities*. New Brunswick: Rutgers U Press, 2001.

Websites:
abseconlighthouse.org
acmuseum.net
atlanticcitynj.com
boardwalkhall.com
cemeteryguide.com
cityofatlanticcity.org
civilwarmusic.net
ettc.net
everyculture.com
findagrave.com
iloveac.com
leslieflint.com
lucytheelephant.org
njlhs.org
oed.com
playbill.com
prairieghosts.com
roadsideamerica.com
steelpier.com
theshadowlands.net
tripadvisor.com
visitnjshore.com
westfieldnj.com

Newspapers:
Atlantic City Weekly
The Philadelphia Inquirer
The Philadelphia Record
The Press of Atlantic City

Interviews:
Anne Brennan
Bob Washington

Photographs of modern-day Atlantic City and environs by Kevin D. Margitich. A very special thanks to Kevin for his invaluable input, for reading and re-reading, for exploring Atlantic City with me, and for finding enjoyment in discovering weird things.

A heartfelt thanks to Tim Reeser and Eileen Reeser for reading, discussing, critiquing, and inspiring...and for our unique dinner conversations. Muchas gracias to Doug Reeser for all of the moral support.

And thank you to the members of my family who called Atlantic City home and must have led me to write about this wacky, wicked place.